SIMPLE ★ SUSTAINABLE ★ DELICIOUS

GRILLING

WHERE THERE'S SMOKE

BARTON SEAVER

STERLING EPICURE
New York

STERLING EPICURE
New York

An Imprint of Sterling Publishing
387 Park Avenue South
New York, NY 10016

ISBN 978-1-4027-9705-7

Library of Congress Cataloging-in-Publication Data

Seaver, Barton.
  Where there's smoke: simple, sustainable, delicious,
  grilling / Barton Seaver.
    pages cm
  ISBN 978-1-4027-9705-7
  1. Barbecuing. I. Title.
  TX840.B3S3926 2013
  641.7′6—dc23

                             2012037560

Distributed in Canada by Sterling Publishing
ᶜ/o Canadian Manda Group, 165 Dufferin Street
Toronto, Ontario, Canada M6K 3H6
Distributed in the United Kingdom by GMC Distribution Services
Castle Place, 166 High Street, Lewes, East Sussex, England BN7 1XU
Distributed in Australia by Capricorn Link (Australia) Pty. Ltd.
P.O. Box 704, Windsor, NSW 2756, Australia

For information about custom editions, special sales, and premium and corporate purchases,
please contact Sterling Special Sales at 800-805-5489 or specialsales@sterlingpublishing.com.

Manufactured in China

2 4 6 8 10 9 7 5 3 1

www.sterlingpublishing.com

Contents

To Hal and Tim—

for helping us to write the most wonderful chapter of our lives.

Acknowledgments

My thanks to

My lovely ladyfish Carrie Anne, Michael and Sean Dimin, Julia Nicolaysen, Cheryl Dahle, Colleen Howell, Bev Eggleston, the Croxton Family at Rappahanock River Oyster Co., Hog Island Oyster Company, Taylor Shellfish, Island Creek Oyster Co., Nic Farias, Myra Goodman, Alicia and Andy Sokol, Fred and Susan Massie at Terrapin View Farm, Nate Anda at Red Apron, Vicki Reh, Gail Ross, Howard Yoon, Robert Egger, Seth and Caroline Hurwitz, Will and Rachel Caggiano (for enduring a little too much heat in the recipe testing), Katie Stoops, Will and Karen, Steve Vilnit, Jeff and Sandy, Amy Witherly, and Dad, the grill master.

Introduction

Why I Grill

I grew up in a family that knew how to eat. Every night we gathered around the table, all of us, putting aside the tasks of our day to come together. The rough clang of the dinner bell was the last prompt, but more often than not, the aromas that filled the house were enough to draw me to the kitchen. That was on the rare days when I wasn't already there, helping to prepare the meal.

In our home, food was participatory, it was uniting, and it was delicious. Meals were never too complicated, a style I initially rebelled against when I first started creating dishes in a restaurant—always adding five unnecessary ingredients. We were lucky in that we were able to choose what we ate for dinner. This was not because we were spoiled or picky children, but rather because we helped do the shopping, we helped prepare the meal, and we ate our vegetables (mostly with joy, I might add). We had all the food we needed, and we were lucky for that. Many of the kids that I knew were not so fortunate.

I was taught to recognize the value of food from the beginning, at first in the simple understanding that there were those who didn't have enough or any. But once I had left the nest, I began to recognize the value of the gifts that I had been given: the love of food, of meals, and of communion. Food was a part of me, and it was how I communicated with the world. I remember throwing dinner parties long before I had a living space that could accommodate the task, seeking to re-create the comfort of the gatherings my parents hosted.

I realized that I was looking to food to feed a more complicated hunger, seeking to nourish with more than calories. I was feeding my need for community, friendship, love, sense of self, and much more. Food was my inheritance, an heirloom passed on by my parents for me to use as I saw fit. My parents taught me the fluency and gave me the capacity to nourish.

How well I remember a meal my father made on a sandy beach below a great-aunt's house in Pugwash, Nova Scotia. We had spent the day waiting at the docks for the lobster boats to come in with their catch. With lobsters in hand after a very easy negotiation, we set off back to the beach to gather seaweed brought in with the tide. There we found mussels hanging from the rocks, ripe for the plucking. Clams were to be had with little more effort than the turning of the spade in the sand.

A driftwood fire was made in a dug-out pit, and the seaweed and seafood were piled in and buried.

Puzzled as to how this was going to turn out, I went back to my playing. My brother dared me to jump up and put my chin on the clothesline, a challenge I confidently accepted. A few hours later, the cut on my tongue was still throbbing from where my teeth had chomped down on it with the full weight of my body on that clothesline. You still owe me for that one, brother! But the sweet and unbelievably fresh seafood was more balm than I needed in order to take my thoughts far away from the red mark under my chin. Dad didn't have to build that pit; a simple pot would have sufficed. But there was joy in the seaweed-smothered flames of that fire. Even though it was added effort, the participation in the method made our meal all the more delicious. Many of my favorite memories involve food, the very best of those involve fire.

I can easily recall the scent of a just-lit fire in our small Weber grill in our very tiny urban backyard. My childhood home had a fenced-in area that never saw direct sunlight. There was a dogwood tree, its musky jasmine-like scent adding to the dank aura of moss-covered bricks as the gassy smell of lighter fluid ripened sweetly alongside that of burning charcoal. Grilling was an event with our family, and one worth attending. Dad was a genius with his grilled lamb, chicken legs, corn on the cob, oysters, and homemade peach ice cream. Fresh air and the change of setting were a nice break from the usual dinner-table scenario. Not only were the flavors bolder, but the cooking method also was a part of the meal. The lamb would hit the grill, charring and puffing out smoke as the backyard perfume grew more complex. One of us boys would begin to churn the old hand-crank ice cream machine, with family friends Patsy and

Jeff carefully monitoring the rock-salt-to-ice ratio. Corn was shucked, and the vegetables simply sliced and presented. By the time the lamb came off the grill, the ice cream would be ready for the freezer. Once our bellies were stuffed, we would run in the eventide light, chasing after the fireflies in the alley and plucking honeysuckle flowers, pulling the stamen to gather that one tiny droplet of nectar. That bit of sweetness would remind us of the peach ice cream that was waiting.

When I got my own place, one of the first things I bought was an 18-inch Weber grill. It has stuck with me since, becoming in its own way an heirloom of my early years, as it has seen all the places that I have lived. It has been a

trusty friend and continues to serve me as well as it did on its first day—as a similar grill served my childhood and the memories of those flavors inspire me still.

In this book you will find some of the recipes I have described here. You will find the same spirit of gathering—the joy of a meal shared and received. And there is no better way to arouse this hunger for communion in people than with that first fragrant whiff of smoke, the curling shimmer of heat rising from a grill as the day's swelter fades, a cool drink in hand, friends and family around. Grilling is inherently seasonal, celebratory, and social. We should be so fortunate as to interpret the rest of our lives in the same way.

The Mechanics of Grilling

Fuel for Your Fire: Charcoal Briquettes or Lump Charcoal?

I have used both types of fuel regularly for years now and have to say that I greatly prefer the briquettes. They burn evenly, and those labeled "hardwood" or "natural" have no chemical additives. I like briquettes because I always know what I am going to get—smooth, even-burning, predictable heat. They may not produce as much smoke flavor as lump charcoal, but I make up for that by adding wood chunks or chips to every fire I cook over (for more on this, see Adding Flavor Through Smoke, page 19).

When buying briquettes, do not get the quick-burning kind. And never use lighter fluid—its taste is chemical and lingering. Instead, invest in a chimney lighter; if you do, newspaper is all you will ever need to get your fire going (see Lighting Charcoal, page 14).

As for lump charcoal, it has its benefits. It burns hotter and has more flavor than briquettes. But it burns so quickly and inconsistently that you have to adapt to its pace. Charcoal, by its nature, is an inconsistent-size product. So, by the time the smaller lumps have burned to embers, other larger lumps will still be black and burning raw and acrid. Then there is the problem of the bits at the bottom. You pay for those charcoal crumbs, the same price as the large lump, but they are only a disaster waiting to happen. Lump charcoal can spit, burst, spray fiery embers all over—your shirt, your deck, your food. So while lump charcoal is great for slow-cooked barbecue prepared in an offset smoker, it isn't my first choice for a small grill.

GAS GRILLS

I am a fan of live-fire cooking. I know there is a great debate about the virtues of gas versus charcoal grilling, and I am sympathetic to both camps. Gas grills are far more convenient in terms of initial preparation. But that's where the obvious benefits cease. A gas grill simply cannot create the same deep flavor that a wood-spiked charcoal-fueled fire can. And though there is good proof that gas grills produce meals that are healthier vis-à-vis carcinogen buildup (see page 27), much of the risk of live-fire cooking can be mitigated by a conscientious cook.

The honest truth is that I flat-out prefer grilling over a charcoal fire, and the recipes in this book were developed with a live fire in mind, both in terms of their steps and their flavor. Some of these dishes may not taste as balanced if not supported by a smoky tone. So to get the most from this book if you're using a gas grill, dedicate one portion of the grill to creating a smoke station, an area where you can put a handful of wood chips in aluminum foil and slowly heat them until they smolder. This will add a whiff of smoke to the foods while maintaining the convenience of the gas cooking.

Lighting Charcoal

The charcoal chimney is an indispensable tool that should accompany every live-fire grill. Lighter fluid is jam-packed with all sorts of nasty things, most of which you do not want to ingest. While most of them burn off, some compounds linger and are passed on to the food. This results in a brash, unpleasant chemical aroma.

The chimney needs only a few pages of yesterday's news and a match to get your charcoal flaming. It has an ingenious design that concentrates heat while maximizing airflow to burn the charcoal down to coals rapidly and with no off-tasting additives.

How Big a Fire?

There are too many variables in grilling for me to give strict directions for building your fire: the way the wind blows (if at all), the humidity, the size and make of your grill, and so on. All these factors act in concert and call for a site-specific approach. What may heat my little 18-inch grill to blazing hot might not even warm your grill. So the best way to communicate the levels of fire is to talk in terms of size. Size equates to heat level and is relative to the area of the grill. Thirty briquettes in my grill would make it near impossible for me to create an indirect heat area. In a 27-inch grill, that same number isn't enough to provide the heat you may need for an initial hot sear.

Here is how I equate size with heat:

A small fire = low heat. You can hold your hand comfortably directly above the coals for 4 to 6 seconds.

A medium fire = medium heat. You should bristle after 2 to 3 seconds of direct exposure.

A large fire = very hot. You should think twice about sticking your hand anywhere near it.

Again, all of this is relative to *your* grill, and so you must take the opportunity to learn from your fires. No recipe can ever replace paying attention and knowing your tools.

Indirect Grilling

There are some exceptions, but in most of my recipes, you'll find me instructing you *not* to cook directly over your fire. Instead, you'll be asked to set the food adjacent to the coals or even as far away from the coals as possible.

Fire itself is very difficult to manage. By putting all the coals to one side, you can best leverage the varying grades of heat required in cooking simply by moving your ingredients closer to or farther from the coals. And it creates a more efficient fire by concentrating the heat.

By building your fire so the coals are all on one side of the grill, you can create an environment within the closed grill that is conducive to slow, even cooking. This is similar to the low and slow method of barbecuing, in which the heat source is kept entirely separate from what is being cooked in an offset smoker. This is my preferred method for delicate seafood as well as for whole birds and large steaks that require long cooking. The slower burn and lower temperatures allow for greater penetration of smoke flavor, although you do sacrifice the deep crust gained from a high-heat sear.

The Importance of Airflow

This is one of the only tools you have at your disposal to control fire. The heat, flavor, and duration of your fire all depend on the amount of air it gets during the burn. My grill is set up with an adjustable airflow underneath the fire that also allows for the ashes to be removed.

When the intake is wide open, the fire is burning at full capacity. This is what you want when you first light the fire, to enable the charcoal to burn down to embers as fast as possible. Once this stage is reached, though, this is not necessarily the best use of the charcoal. I rarely recommend cooking over high heat, and so a fire of this intensity is not needed.

By closing the intake at least halfway, you slow the burn rate down, providing a more even heat and a longer burn time. When the intake is closed to just a sliver, the fire is being starved and begins to cool down, providing, as it does, a very mellow and controlled heat.

Covering Your Grill

Covering the grill keeps the heat in, making the most of the energy the fire produces, which allows for lower-temperature fires. Lower temperature equals more control. It is far easier to remove the cover to cool down a grill than it is to cool down a raging pile of coals.

I admit, though, that there is an odd cult of the masculine that has grown up around the grill. The primal scent of sizzle gathers folks in hypnotized fashion to stare at the coals and covet the grill master's tongs. Grilling is a participatory cooking method. But when the grill is covered, ingredients cooking away, and the grill master confident in his movements, the grill puffs and whispers of what is to come. This is far sexier, I think, than a billowing plume of smoke. Think of it as you do perfume. Do you want to be enveloped in an overpowering cloud of scent? Or do you want to have your head turned, attention tickled by a slight, faint but intoxicating smell whose source you must know? Tempt and torture your friends with this. And at the same time, get the most out of your fire.

INDIRECT HEAT ON A GAS GRILL

Indirect grilling over gas is simple enough to mimic. Almost all gas grills have at least two sections of heating units that are separately controlled.

Light one side to low heat and the other to high. If you have more zones than that, you may not need to light them all, or you can set them at gradually lower levels. You must, however, cover your grill and keep it covered.

Techniques of Grilling

Adding Flavor Through Smoke

Smoke is the reason I grill. I adore the soulful and sultry appeal of the aroma and glistening caramel color of food just removed from a flavorful fire. In my restaurants, I always cooked over wood fires in massive grills.

Smoke, to my mind, is an ingredient, as basic as stock or olive oil. It is foundational in its presence in a dish. When used well, it adds richness and fullness to the inherent flavors of the foods it touches. But smoke can also overpower if not managed properly.

Wood smoke goes through different phases as it billows from a fire. At lower burning temperatures, between 550 and 700 degrees F, it is pillowy and friendly, complex and reflective of its source. As the wood reaches higher temperatures, the smoke changes flavors because different compounds are released or created. It can still be very flavorful and pretty in its aromas.

But it is the low smoke, the celebratory release of bound energy, decades of sunlight turned to flavor, that is most sought after and best accentuates food.

All smoke is not the same. Different woods have unique characteristics that can be paired with foods in different ways. Softwoods such as pine are not good for smoking, as they have high resin content and burn unevenly and with unappetizing flavors. Hardwoods such as oak and maple are the most commonly used smoking woods. Woods like mesquite that are high in lignan, a cellular component of wood, burn very hot and sometimes with aggressive flavors. Others, such as orchard woods of fruit or nut trees, burn more slowly and can have very subtle and sweet undertones. Also, depending on the chemical makeup of the wood, some offer more aromatic compounds, while others add more flavor components. Whether the wood has bark on it or not can also affect the flavor it generates. I prefer the stronger flavor of bark wood, as I think it is more representative of the tree. Some barbecue purists who are cooking their meat for twenty-four hours or more find that the bark flavor becomes too strong over time. A quick-cook item, though, is not going to be adversely affected. Cooking with wood is a game of near endless possibilities, one worth playing, and easy to win.

A Few of My Favorite Woods

Here are some of my favorites, but I am always experimenting with anything new I can find. There are a number of online sources for buying woods (see Sources, page 296). Be aware that some woods are poisonous, so don't go around smoking whatever you can find—this isn't high school. And never use chemically treated wood or lumber, as it can impart some nasties to your food and to you.

Alder: This is the traditional smoking wood of the Pacific Northwest. It has a very clean, cool scent with a lingering sweetness. It is best used with seafood, specifically salmon, and poultry.

Apple: I think that this is the tangiest of the fruitwoods, and it is certainly the most popular. It imparts a sweet, ashy flavor and is particularly good with pork and poultry.

Cherry: This wood is high on aroma and lighter on flavor than other fruitwoods. I have noticed that it gives more color to foods than many other woods. It imparts a whiff of clove scent and pairs well with seafood and poultry. I think it is at its best when mixed with other fruitwoods and goes especially well with fatty pork.

Citrus: This includes lemon, orange, and grapefruit woods. I have never used lime wood, so I cannot comment on that. These woods all show very similar character and are surprisingly mild, given the tart fruit the trees bear. They are best paired with vegetables and poultry.

Hickory: This is one of the strongest woods I have encountered. It has a deep flavor that is seemingly viscous and coating to the palate. I like it best with hamburgers, fatty beef cuts, and lean pork cuts like tenderloin. Hickory can be very bitter if burned too hot, so be mindful with airflow to the fire.

Maple: Maple offers the most classic smoke in terms of the balance between bitter and sweet. It perfectly contrasts the earthy flavor of wood and the soaring aroma of billowing smoke, leaving a whisper of the flavor of maple syrup. Use it for flavorful seafood such as lobster or salmon; it also pairs nicely with pork and beef.

Mesquite: This is the wood of the Southwest and a common flavoring smoke for Tex-Mex cuisine. I find it to be very powerful, and it can be aggressive to a fault. This wood burns very hot and so a little bit can go a long way. I think mesquite is best used with foods that include chile peppers, cilantro, and/or cumin.

Oak: For long-smoke items, this is the best wood. It has a mild, woodsy flavor with a hint of vanilla and citrus rind that pairs well with all meats and many types of seafood. It can also be blended with stronger woods. If you use only one kind of wood, this should be it.

Peach: Just like the fruit of the tree, peach wood is the queen of the category. It produces an elegant and charming light-flavored smoke with spice and ashy notes. Although the smoke is light, it flavors well and combines with other flavors seamlessly, especially fresh herbs and dry spices. This is best for seafood—especially shellfish, poultry, and pork.

Pecan: I use pecan in place of hickory often, as it delivers some of that same musky character but is tempered with a sweet, nutty aroma and less bitterness.

Whiskey barrel staves: These are usually made of heavily charred oak, and when burned, they exhibit the muscular and elegant scent of the barrel's former contents. This pairs nicely with ribs and fatty pork.

Wine barrel staves: These are also usually made from oak and deliver much of the same character as straight oak. However, in the first few minutes of smoking, you can detect notes of the wine lingering in the wood. I use this for its super-fruity, boozy flavor and usually only with cold-smoking and low-temperature cooking, to prolong the initial flavors of the wine.

Chips, Chunks, Sticks, and Dust

When adding wood to flavor your fire, the type of wood isn't the only choice you can make. The form that wood takes can also have an effect on the food you're grilling.

Wood chips are high on surface area and low on volume. These can be added to a charcoal fire to give a more lasting smoke flavor than sawdust. They do add a bit of heat, so it is important to adjust the placement of your ingredients if necessary.

Wood chunks are the best way to get long-lasting heat and flavor into a meal. They burn slowly when choked for air and deliver a heady smoke. When given a little airflow, wood chunks will replace some charcoal (or all of it, if desired) and provide a good amount of heat.

Sticks are not often used in cooking, but I love to collect a few armfuls whenever I am at an orchard to have on hand for the grilling months. The sticks need to be dried for at least a few months so that they are not resinous and off tasting. Why use them at all? Because they have a very high ratio of bark to volume. In most cases the bark is a more powerful flavor than the wood, and sometimes this is perfect. The burning bark imparts an ashy taste to food. Too much of this is too much, but it is a different flavor and one that I enjoy in some dishes.

Sawdust is best when you want to deliver a slight hint of flavor to a food without creating any additional heat. This is great in gas grills, as it will fill the chamber with smoke but not cause any hot spots.

To Soak or Not to Soak

I always accepted that soaking wood before adding it to a fire had some effect and so did it when it was convenient. But when it wasn't soaked, I never really noticed any difference in the smoke that was produced. So I tried something. I soaked wood chips and chunks overnight and then cut them in half to see how deeply the water had actually penetrated. The answer was not at all. In the chips, where there is a greater surface area, they were noticeably wet, but not saturated.

When adding wood to a fire, the purpose is to add flavor, and the purpose of the fire is to create heat. There is great nuance in smoke at its many stages. But water does not really affect this; in fact, it just delays the heating process. Soaked wood only cools the fire, and makes managing the heat more difficult. Wood combusts at around 575 degrees F, so if you soak the wood, you need to steam off all the water before it can reach its prime smoking temperature. I don't see the point; skip the soak.

Beyond Wood

Remember that smoke doesn't have to come from wood! I also like to use dried herbs (if you grow your own herbs, at the end of the season, you can pull up the plants, hang them to dry, and then use them as flavor fuel), spices (cinnamon sticks, star anise pods), and tea leaves with great effect.

I also like to use fennel stalks. When you buy fennel, you usually use the bulb and throw the stalks away. But when air-dried, those brittle stalks become highly aromatic, with a heady anise and honey scent. They are best used as a base for food to rest on and to buffer the heat of the fire. Place the stalks on the grill grate and then any kind of fish fillet directly on top. As the stalks smolder from the rising heat, they release their aroma but do not combust.

Development of Flavor in Grilled Proteins

There is a common idea held by cooks everywhere that searing a protein creates an impermeable layer that "locks in the juices." This process of browning, known as the Maillard reaction, is what changes the flavor and texture of the protein involved, giving it a complex and primal appeal. But it does not lock in the juices—nothing can lock in juices. We can only hope to retain as much of a food's natural moisture as possible through the use of tempered heat and proper resting.

So why do we sear proteins? For flavor. We have come to prefer meat with a dark crust, slightly bitter and elemental in flavor. But when cooking with really good-quality meat or fish, this is unnecessary and, in fact, too much browning can ruin the nuanced flavor of the food. A little char is fine, but the art of grilling is more than just the application of heat. It is the application of flavorful heat, best when allowed to slowly permeate the protein.

You will notice in my recipes that in most cases I call for the proteins to be cooked away from or just adjacent to the coals for the majority of the time. Good cooking is all about balance of flavors—and good grilling is the balance of heat and smoke.

Flipping Meat on the Grill

I am always amazed when I watch cooks on TV constantly messing with whatever it is they are cooking. Tossing sauté pans deep in the burners to create big plumes of fire, flipping, stirring, fiddling. But I guess that actual cooking, the transfer of heat into ingredients, is not so entertaining because it happens at a molecular level. It's the drama and action we want to see!

And this is also common to home cooks, but I think less so for the drama than because of a lack of confidence. Food does not need to be messed with. Just let it be and allow the heat to work its magic.

Flipping is important, though, when grilling, more to ensure even cooking than for any aesthetic purpose. Developing nice crosshatch marks from the grates is a fine thing, but most of the cooking in my recipes does not call for direct searing, so this is not really an issue.

The flipping that you should do is aimed at achieving even, gentle penetration of the food with heat from both sides. This even cooking allows for greater moisture retention and better flavor. Most of the time with fish, I never call for flipping because of its delicate nature. With meat, two to three flips are usually enough.

Think of flipping like steering a car. In order to maintain a forward course, it requires constant slight corrections of the wheel rather than a huge pull to the right, then a huge pull to the left. When cooking, the heat should be manipulated in the same way, a moderate amount applied to one side, and then alternating to the other to give the heat an easy path toward the center. Just a few repetitions of this cycle, and the meat will be evenly cooked and juicy.

And remember, every time you use tongs or a spatula, even with the utmost care, you are squeezing or pressing the meat, thus expelling juices, or breaking the surface of the meat, causing a loss of moisture.

Cooking Multiple Courses on One Fire

When preparing a meal outside on the grill, you have to think a little bit about how the flow will go. It requires some planning to decide how each grilled item will cook and what can be made ahead. In this book you will find that most of the dishes are equally good when served hot or at room temperature.

When the fire is built, the coals burning with a shimmering orange glow, the smoke of added wood chunks pouring out, you need a plan of action for how to make the most of it. Many of the proteins in this book call for indirect heat cooking, leaving the space over the coals open for crisping kale, searing shaved fennel, charring young tender carrots. The point is that you have a vast array of options. Say you have four to six burners on the stove in your kitchen; you are simmering this soup on low, boiling that vegetable on high, high-heat sautéing on the front burner, and warming a sauce in the back. We understand this approach to cooking. The

grill is exactly the same and can be arranged so that many things can happen at once, all at different temperatures. Yes, it does require some skill and attention—a difficult task when friends arrive and spirits are high (and flowing).

Choose a number of dishes to make ahead and serve at room temperature. Then craft a sequence for the fire. Cook your steak, initially searing it over high heat, then slowly roasting it away from the fire as you move fennel directly over the coals. When the steaks have been removed and are resting, reheat spaghetti squash or garlic bread so that when the steak is ready to be sliced, so too are the sides ready to be served, piping hot off the grill. As you sit down to dinner, place some ripe peaches over the dying embers and choke the fire.

When the meal is cleared, uncover the grill to reveal beautifully dark caramelized peaches infused with the deep, soulful, smoky exhalations of a dying fire. Top them with vanilla ice cream and a drizzle of balsamic, and there you have it.

Of one fire, many dishes, each with unique character. That is the mark of a skilled grill cook.

Carrie Anne, my beautiful wife

Hal, our beloved friend who introduced me to my wife

Techniques for Healthier and Greener Grilling

There are some very real concerns associated with cooking over live fire. A good amount of chemical reaction occurs in the process of combustion, making it the least clean form of cooking. But the compounds that are formed and released are also the source of the unique flavor we seek when cooking on a grill. So I urge you to make an informed choice about the impacts of grilling and to take steps to mitigate them.

Carbon dioxide: Grilling releases an appreciable quantity of this greenhouse gas. Propane gas grilling results in the lowest output, as it burns cleanest. Generally the preheating time is shorter than that of charcoal, and it can be turned off immediately after cooking.

Charcoal results in roughly double the output of carbon emissions. Still, this amount is negligible compared with other daily activities such as driving and the production of the food that we are grilling. And there are ways to minimize this output. Use natural charcoal with no lighter fluid and no chemical binders. Light the charcoal in a chimney starter fueled by crumpled newspaper. And when you are done cooking, starve the fire completely of oxygen to stop it from burning.

No matter how you're grilling, carbon emissions can be further reduced simply by electing to serve a small portion of protein alongside lots of vegetables. The positive impact of reduced meat consumption far outweighs the minimal impact of a small fire. This also has some very real health benefits.

Carcinogens: The combustion of wood or charcoal releases not only carbon, but also a host of rather undesirable things. Chief among them is a buildup of heterocyclic amines (HCA) in meat. This is due to naturally present compounds in animal protein that become carcinogenic when subjected to high heat. However, this is easily avoided. Most of the recipes in this book call for cooking away from direct heat over a slow and tempered fire. This alone greatly reduces the danger, and it also gives credence to another suggestion in this book: cook one large cut for many people, as opposed to many individual portions. By greatly reducing the surface area of the animal protein on the grill, you drastically reduce the production of these nasty HCAs. The surface of meat is the only part that reaches temperatures high enough to cause damage—the less surface area, the less risk. And there are other benefits, too. One large portion cooks more slowly, requiring a lower-temperature fire (and a lot less charcoal), thereby cutting risk. And I believe that one large cut, cooked beautifully and then sliced super thin, reduces the amount of protein your guests will consume, as there is greater taste appreciation with respect to portion size. Less meat served and less charcoal burned means fewer carbon emissions, a win-win.

When the fat of animal protein is subjected to high heat, it can burn and transform into another carcinogen called polyaromatic hydrocarbon (PAH). This, again, is easily avoided by cooking away from the fire and by choosing leaner cuts or trimming away unnecessary fat. External fat, such as that which covers one side of a strip steak, does not have much culinary virtue to begin with, so just get rid of it before cooking.

Are these solutions absolute? No. There are always some negative impacts in cooking, almost all forms of cooking. And be aware that we subject ourselves to a host of carcinogens every day in the products we use. There are PAHs in some shampoos, metals in some deodorants, carcinogens in some sunblock lotions meant to block cancer-causing radiation, residual pesticides in food grown using conventional agricultural methods. I am not an alarmist, but everything that we do, every product we use, has impacts. I just ask that you be mindful and purposeful in how you use this information.

Wines for the Grill

Many wine experts have given advice on what to pair with grilled foods, and I have learned quite a lot from their suggestions. But I have to say that most of their ideas are based on the assumption that grilled foods are sweet, which in this country they often are. Bottled BBQ sauces are nothing more than spiced sugar in varying viscosities. This has profound effect on wines. But the recipes in this book are decidedly not bathed in a sugar coating. The other complication in pairing wine with grilled foods is that the smoke flavor can be overwhelming. But read through my recipes and you will find that I use smoke in a more nuanced fashion, as a seasoning to help round out other flavors and accentuate the grilled ingredients.

This, too, is the purpose of wine. Sure, it has alcohol in it, and you can drink it just to have fun. And certainly you can renounce trying to pair food and wine and just drink what you like (which I actually encourage to a large extent). But you can also use wine to elevate the experience.

Food is complex. In this book I write of the differences in varieties of beef, of the differences in flavors of wood and charcoal, of seasonings, of presalting or not, of resting meats, and of many other details. Each of these things has some import as to the wine pairing that will support it best. There is only one rule that guarantees success, however, and that is to drink what you want, eat what you want. So I do not attempt to give explicit instructions for exact pairings, only broad suggestions based on general flavors common to each.

Wines with Grass-fed Beef

Zinfandel is probably the most commonly suggested wine to pair with grilled foods. I disagree. Can it be good? Yes. But zinfandel typically is a brutish, flamboyant, over-the-top Miami Beach body builder of a wine—ostentatious, flashy, and overdone. The alcohol content of zins typically teeters on the edge of classifying them as a spirit. And high alcohol content can leave a searing, hot taste on the palate, no matter how much fruit there is. This quality can be magnified by the smoke in grilled foods.

But a really good zin can be a spectacular treat. Ask your wine seller for a muted, cooler-climate zin, one that delivers balance, not bulge. When a zin is well crafted, it still has muscle but with an extremely charming blackberry and smoke character. It is low in acid and pairs particularly well with grass-fed beef, helping to mellow its characteristic tangy aftertaste.

When grilling grass-fed beef, also try the confident flavors of *barbera*, an Italian variety from the Piedmont region. These wines display soft character with low tannin and a crescendo of acidity. I have found that sometimes the wine can nearly disappear on the palate when paired with grass-fed beef, but it sure makes the beef taste good. Also, give *dolcetto* and *Ribera del Duero* wines a shot. And most all of these pair nicely with grilled lamb.

Wines with Fatty Cuts of Beef

These need a partner that is a little more assertive. Again, a lower-alcohol *zinfandel* can be beautiful, especially when the steak is slowly smoked using a light-tasting fruitwood like cherry. *Syrah*, with distinguishing black pepper flavor and reserved fruit aromas, is another favorite of mine. This French wine pairs well with the broad flavors of fatty beef, as its flavors can be quite punctuated on the palate, thus bringing a sense of focus to the meal. I find that Washington State *merlots* complement slow-grilled fatty steaks very nicely. They do not so much provide a counterpoint to the flavors as cheer them on, mimicking them, reflecting them, which can be a pretty bold experience.

Wines with Pork

You can go white or red. The Pork Council has spent so much money trying to convince us that pork is the other white meat that we sort of have to acknowledge its versatility. Lighter style *pinot noirs* from cooler climates such as the coastal areas in Sonoma County, California, and Willamette Valley in Oregon tend to be very smoke- and fat-friendly.

Pork-friendly whites represent a broad array of flavors, and they are easier to get right than to go wrong. My favorites are *chenin blanc*, *viognier*, and full-bodied styles of *sauvignon blanc*.

A Broad Selection of Grill-Friendly Wines

For nearly everything else that one could conceivably grill—from rich, sweet autumn squash to a simple chicken breast or fish fillet—there are a few wines I find nearly universally accommodating.

Cool-climate pinot noirs: These wines are rarely aggressive and tend to play a good supporting role.

Cru beaujolais (red): The *gamay* grape makes fantastic and sometimes hauntingly beautiful wines. Its good name, though, has been tarnished by its unruly little brother, Beaujolais Nouveau. While made from the same grape, the nouveau-style wines use a different fermentation technique, resulting in a very simple wine that holds up only for a few months and is the source of much revelry and debauchery every November when it is released. When grown in better soils and treated with great care, the quietly noble gamay can produce wines of great complexity, nuance, fruit, acid, and ageability. There are ten *crus*, or villages, that make wines of distinct character from gamay. Each is worth investigating, and the prices are often quite reasonable.

Chenin blanc: This white wine is remarkably versatile. It has a wonderful balance of rich, sweet aromas of apricot and green plum, but also a mineral austerity that creates a lovely harmony. It does seem to have a specter of sweetness detectable on the finish, but this is what really brings the smoke in grilled foods to life. It works as well with pork as it does with chicken, vegetables, and seafood. This is my go-to grill wine.

Lightly oaked sauvignon blanc: Of all the grapes grown around the world, this one displays the greatest range of tastes—many of which I don't care for, I must say. At its worst, this wine can be overwhelming, with a scent that evokes a lawn mower chewing through equal parts overripe summer grass and unripe apples.

But when sauvignon blanc balances its defining green aromas of grass, hay, and citrus, it is something to behold. The classic growing region of Sancerre in France produces wines from this grape of extraordinary character and grace. But they are not grill-friendly in the least. You want to look for a tame California version that has been mellowed by a touch of oak aging. This will coax the sweetness from the wood flavors of grilled foods and accentuate everything from vegetables to fatty pork.

And a Few Surprises

Dry Amontillado sherry: This fortified wine from the south of Spain is profoundly good with grilled fatty seafood like salmon and bluefish. It has a deep, nutty tone of candied walnuts and boiling honey, and the dry version lacks the associated sweetness but packs great acidity. I particularly love this with Grilled Pork Shoulder Steak with Pickled Peach and Chile Chutney (page 243).

Verdelho Madeira: Madeira is widely considered a dessert wine. It is fortified and, yes, it tends to be sweet. But there are styles worth asking around about, and my favorite is the verdelho. In this wine, the fermentation is stopped just before all the sugars have been fermented, leaving a touch of sweetness but with a high acidity and smoky almond notes that make for a charismatic drink. This pairs particularly well with sweet Pacific Coast oysters and aromatic vegetables like fennel and grilled carrots. It can also be an interesting dance partner for grilled fatty pork. One doesn't quite know what dance step they are performing, but it works.

WINE SALTS

These salts are a fun way to season just about anything on the grill to help match it to the wine you are drinking. Use these salts just as you would regular salt or any of the meat-specific salts. These work just as well on meats as they do on vegetables and are a way to introduce complementary flavors to spark the wines. The combinations are not exact, and there are certainly great differences in how a single variety of grape tastes when grown in different regions. But in general, the flavors are relatively consistent. You will need to follow your gut on what to pair each of these with. Sprinkling Zinfandel Salt on a raw clam isn't necessarily going to make zinfandel wine any more appropriate a pairing.

Sauvignon Blanc Salt

2 tablespoons kosher salt

4 celery seeds

Finely shredded zest of ½ lemon

2 fresh mint leaves

½ teaspoon smoked sweet paprika

Combine ½ tablespoon of the salt and the remaining ingredients in a mortar and grind to a powder with a pestle. Add the remaining salt and mix well. Use within a few hours.

Chardonnay Salt

2 tablespoons kosher salt

Pinch ground allspice

½ teaspoon ground coriander

½ teaspoon ground cinnamon

Finely shredded zest of ½ orange

Leaves from 1 sprig fresh tarragon

Combine all the ingredients in a small bowl and mix with your fingers, gently bruising the tarragon leaves to release their aromatic oils. Cover and let sit for at least 20 minutes; use within a few hours.

Pinot Grigio Salt

2 tablespoons kosher salt

1 teaspoon ground fennel seeds

1 thumbnail-size piece fresh ginger, peeled and grated on a Microplane or very finely minced

½ teaspoon ground allspice

Combine all the ingredients and mix well. Use within a day or two.

Riesling Salt

2 tablespoons kosher salt

3 fresh mint leaves

Leaves from 1 sprig fresh thyme

4 caraway seeds

Finely shredded zest of 1 lime

4 food-grade dried rose petals or 2 drops rosewater (optional)

Take ½ tablespoon of the salt and combine it with the remaining ingredients in a mortar; grind to a powder with a pestle. Add the remaining salt and mix well. Let sit at least 20 minutes; use within a few hours.

Viognier Salt

2 tablespoons kosher salt

1 star anise pod, grated on a Microplane or pulverized with a mortar and pestle

1 teaspoon ground mace

1 thumbnail-size piece fresh ginger, peeled and grated on a Microplane or very finely minced

1 teaspoon dried culinary lavender buds

3 turns freshly ground black pepper

Combine all the ingredients and mix well. Use within a day or two.

Pinot Noir Salt

2 tablespoons kosher salt

1 teaspoon ground fennel seeds

½ teaspoon ground cinnamon

½ teaspoon smoked sweet paprika

2 dried shiitake mushrooms, grated on a Microplane or pulverized with a mortar and pestle

Combine all the ingredients and mix well. Cover and use within a day or two.

Merlot Salt

2 tablespoons kosher salt

4 fresh mint leaves

1 thumbnail-size piece fresh ginger, peeled and grated on a Microplane or very finely minced

1 teaspoon ground marjoram

1 teaspoon ground fennel seeds

4 gratings from a whole nutmeg

3 drops vanilla extract

Mix all the ingredients with your fingers to lightly bruise the mint leaves and release their aromatic oils. Use within a day.

Syrah Salt

2 tablespoons kosher salt

1 teaspoon smoked sweet paprika

½ teaspoon ground cinnamon

½ teaspoon ground cumin

½ teaspoon ground mace

Leaves from 1 sprig fresh thyme

1 teaspoon powdered coffee beans (pulverize in a mortar or coffee grinder)

Mix all the ingredients and let sit at least 1 hour before using. Can be used for up to a week; store in an airtight container.

Zinfandel Salt

2 dried shiitake mushrooms

1 small bay leaf

1 clove

2 tablespoons kosher salt

½ teaspoon ground cinnamon

3 turns coarsely ground black pepper

Finely shredded zest of 1 orange

In a mortar, pulverize the dried shiitakes, bay leaf, and clove together. Transfer to a small container, add the remaining ingredients, and mix well. Use with a few days; keep tightly covered.

Cabernet Sauvignon Salt

2 tablespoons kosher salt

1 bay leaf, pulverized in a mortar

1 teaspoon ground mace

1 teaspoon smoked sweet paprika

3 turns coarsely ground black pepper

2 teaspoons unsweetened cocoa powder

1/3 star anise pod, grated

Mix all the ingredients. Use within a few days; store in an airtight container.

1 WELCOME
Drinks + Starters

Getting a meal off the ground can be a harrying experience, even if it's just for the family, it is enough of a task to plan, arrange, gather, smile—to keep calm and carry on. Then the doorbell rings, and guests arrive!

This is always my favorite moment of the night—when I am forced to stop, take stock of what I have (and have not) accomplished. There is nothing to do at this point but to welcome company and to enjoy. You grab a drink and pour a round for all, grab the matches, and head for the grill to ignite the centerpiece of the meal. Having a couple of recipes for fun and seasonal cocktails can make things much easier.

Snacks are essential, to put your mind (and tummy) at ease and to buy you some time to relax. Many of the recipes in this chapter can be made ahead of time, or else they engage people in the process. There is an intense envy hanging in the air because everyone wants to hold the tongs and fiddle with the fire, so hand them an oyster knife and put them to work to deflect their attention.

I like to go heavy on the early part of the meal and serve a lot of appetizers and easy first courses, as it eases people into the evening. It quiets rumbling bellies, and it gives needed time for the fire to burn down to embers, reflecting the last of the day's light. You can work at your own pace and actually be present with your company.

Blueberry-Mint Spritzer

This is just one of the refreshing drinks my wife and I enjoy all summer long.

Juice of 8 lemons

½ cup blueberries

Leaves from 4 sprigs fresh mint

Ice cubes

2 cups white grape juice

1 liter seltzer or club soda

In a large cocktail shaker, combine the lemon juice, all but a few of the blueberries, the mint, and a handful of ice cubes. Cover and shake vigorously to smash the blueberries and extract the flavor of the mint. Pour the contents into a large pitcher and add 2 cups of ice and the grape juice. Stir to combine. Add the seltzer and garnish with the remaining blueberries. Serve immediately.

BOOZY VERSION: When adding alcohol to this, it's better to use club soda, not seltzer. You can spike this two different ways: Substitute light rum or dry vermouth for 1 cup of the club soda, or substitute sparkling wine for all of the seltzer.

Makes about 2 quarts or 8 drinks

Smoky Maple Syrup Lemonade

Grilling the lemons before juicing them tones down the sweetness and tames the acidity, resulting in a refreshing and balanced drink.

4 Grilled Lemons (page 284)

2 quarts warm water

½ cup maple syrup, or more if needed

Leaves from 3 sprigs fresh mint

1 dried chipotle pepper (optional)

Ice cubes

Fresh lemon juice, if needed

Squeeze the grilled lemons into a pitcher and drop in two of the halves; discard the rest. Add the water, maple syrup, mint, and chipotle if using. Muddle the mixture with a wooden spoon to extract the most flavor from the ingredients. Add ice and stir to combine; chill. Taste to see if the sweet/tart balance is to your liking and adjust with either more maple syrup or a bit of fresh lemon juice. Serve immediately.

BOOZY VERSION: Add 1 ounce Mount Gay rum or vodka to each glass, then pour in the lemonade.

Makes about 2½ quarts or 8 drinks

Mulled Apple Cider

I have found that I enjoy grilling in the cooler months more than I do in the blazing heat of summer. Standing alongside a fire in the cool air of autumn is one of the most relaxing scenarios I can imagine. It's also nice to have a warm drink to fend off the chill, and there is no scent more romantically autumnal than that of mulling cider. There are many ways to make it; this is one I particularly favor. I like to add a little savory spice to keep it from becoming too dessert-like as it reduces.

½ gallon fresh apple cider (I prefer UV to heat pasteurization)

1 lemon, zest peeled in strips, then juiced

1 stick cinnamon

4 cloves

4 allspice berries

2 sprigs fresh thyme

Pinch of kosher salt

Combine all the ingredients in a large saucepan and warm them over low heat. (I prefer to mull the cider slowly, as high heat causes the spices to release a hint of bitter flavor; it also destroys some of the nuance of the cider itself. And if you mull it slowly, your house will smell awesome for hours!)

When the cider is sufficiently warm and the spices have infused their flavor, at least 30 minutes, crank the heat for just 1 minute to get it steaming hot, not boiling. Serve immediately in heatproof mugs.

BOOZY VERSION: If you were to serve me this, I would not complain if there were a dash of brandy or good rum in it.

Serves 4

Black Velvet

It may seem a bit of an odd combination, but this classic cocktail is perfect with oysters.

Two 16-ounce cans Guinness stout, chilled

One 750-ml bottle Champagne (real Champagne is best, but any good-quality sparkling wine will do), chilled

In a tall glass or Champagne flute, pour the stout to fill the glass halfway. You may need to pour twice, letting the foam recede in between, in order to do this.

Once the foam from the stout has receded, gently pour the Champagne down the side of the glass until it is full. If the procedure succeeds, you will have two layers, the dark stout on the bottom, Champagne floating on top. Serve immediately.

Serves 8

Peach and Wheat Beer Shandy

The shandy is a classic drink, made in a multitude of different ways. In the summer, I prefer drinking lightly sweet and highly aromatic wheat beers garnished with a double wedge of lemon. I took that as my starting point for this shandy embellished with a wedge of summer-ripe peach.

½ ripe peach, pitted and peeled with a knife

Juice of ½ lemon

Ice cubes

One 12-ounce bottle wheat beer, chilled

1 peach or lemon wedge for garnish

In a cocktail shaker, combine the peach half, lemon juice, and a few ice cubes. Cover and shake vigorously to crush the peach. Pour the contents into a tall beer glass. Add the wheat beer, pouring slowly to avoid creating too much of a foamy head. Garnish with a peach or lemon wedge and serve immediately.

Serves 1

Preserved Cherry Old-Fashioned

I have always loved an Old-Fashioned, but they were nearly impossible to find in restaurants or bars until recently. The trick is getting the subtle balance of smoky bourbon and scented fruit with just a hint of sugar to bring it all together. In this version I use bourbon-preserved cherries plus a few splashes of the cherry juice-infused bourbon to add extra depth.

2 ounces bourbon or rye

2 dashes Angostura bitters

1 strip orange zest

Ice cubes

1 tablespoon bourbon from Bourbon Cherries (recipe on page 43)

2 Bourbon Cherries for garnish

In a highball glass, combine the bourbon, bitters, orange zest, a few ice cubes, and the cherry-infused bourbon; stir well. Garnish with the cherries and serve.

Serves 1

Bourbon Cherries

In the early summer when cherries first hit the market, I like to grab a few pounds for spiking. I find the early-season cherries have a denser texture and so maintain their form over the long months they are left macerating in booze. And even though these cherries are not as sweet as their late-season counterparts, their aroma is stronger, which yields a better infusion. These cherries can be made with any kind of strong liquor you would use to make a cocktail. For a more mellow tone than the bourbon version, I like to use a good rum such as Gosling's or Mount Gay or even a dark rum like Myers's.

¾ pound fresh cherries, stems removed (nearly any type will do)

1 pint bourbon (plus a little more depending on your container)

Shredded zest of 1 orange

½ cup sugar

4 cloves

1 stick cinnamon

Fill a 1-quart container with the cherries. Combine the bourbon, orange zest, sugar, and cloves in a medium bowl and stir to dissolve the sugar. Wedge the cinnamon stick into the jar, then pour the liquid over to cover. Cover the jar tightly and let it sit for at least 2 months in a cool, dark place. These really get good after about 4 months and will keep for up to a year, as long as the cherries are always submerged in the alcohol. It is not necessary to refrigerate them, but do add more booze if needed to keep them covered.

Makes about 1 quart

Sunny Mary

A good Bloody Mary is a thing of beauty and grace. Though many consign it to weekend brunch, I like it as an afternoon respite, because a Bloody Mary not only takes the edge off the day, but also takes the edge off your appetite as you get closer to dinner.

Bartenders everywhere all have their own secret/special/famous recipes for this drink. And that is what makes a Bloody Mary so much fun. In my version, the base mix is made with fresh, summer-ripe tomatoes, which beats canned tomato juice hands-down for taste and color. I especially like to use yellow tomatoes, as they tend to have a subtler flavor and give the drink a bright, sunny color—hence the name. The base mix, without the booze, also makes for a fantastic pick-me-up in the morning.

DRINK MIX:

1½ pounds yellow heirloom tomatoes such as Lemon Boy, Yellow Brandywine, or a yellow plum, stems removed and cut into large chunks

¼ cup Worcestershire sauce

¼ cup sherry vinegar

2 tablespoons prepared horseradish

Half of one 2-ounce can oil-packed anchovies, about 8 fillets

Juice of 1 lime

Kosher salt

1 tablespoon hot sauce such as Tapatío or Frank's Red Hot (optional)

½ cup extra-virgin olive oil

FOR EACH DRINK:

Ice cubes

1½ ounces vodka

1 fresh basil leaf or pickled wax bean (page 287) for garnish

For the drink mix, combine all the ingredients in a blender and purée on high speed until smooth. Check the seasoning and adjust it if necessary. I do not like to refrigerate this before serving, relying on the ice in the glass to chill it.

For each drink, fill a tall glass with ice. Pour the vodka over the ice, then fill the glass with the base. Stir to combine and garnish with a basil leaf or wax bean. Serve immediately.

Makes about 2 quarts mix (enough for 6 cocktails)

Campari-Watermelon Cocktail

Campari is one of my favorite aperitifs. When mixed correctly, its bitterness can make for a truly mature drink, one that really excites the palate. Campari tends also to be lower in alcohol and so is a gentle way to start a gathering.

1½ ounces Campari

2 ounces seedless fresh-cut watermelon, about two fingers' worth

1 sprig fresh mint

1 teaspoon white balsamic or white wine vinegar

3 to 4 ice cubes

4 ounces club soda

In a cocktail shaker, combine the Campari, half the watermelon, the mint, vinegar, and ice. Cover and shake vigorously to crush the watermelon and extract the flavor of the mint. Pour the contents, unstrained, into a rocks glass. Garnish the rim of the glass with the remaining piece of watermelon and fill the glass with club soda. Serve immediately.

Serves 1

Smoked Peach Manhattan

This is a fun twist on a venerable cocktail. The smokiness of the pickled peach is a perfect partner for the smoky bourbon, actually softening the bourbon's aroma and allowing its nuttier undertones to shine through. I have made this with both sweet and dry vermouth and have enjoyed it both ways. When I use sweet vermouth, though, I like to add a dash of the peach pickle brine to give it an acidic kick.

2 ounces bourbon or rye

½ ounce sweet vermouth (look for Carpano Antica or Dolin Rouge brand)

2 dashes Angostura bitters

1 teaspoon brine from Pickled Smoked Peaches (page 288)

Ice cubes

1 slice Pickled Smoked Peach for garnish

Combine the bourbon, vermouth, bitters, and brine in a cocktail shaker. Add ice and stir to chill. Strain into a martini glass. Garnish with the slice of peach and serve immediately.

Serves 1

White Port Spritzer

White port is not well known in this country, but it deserves a place of honor on any good host's shelf. It is a wonderfully viscous fortified wine that shows colors running from straw to a deep sunset yellow. It is made in Portugal, just like the red port, but I like it best when drunk at the beginning of a meal rather than as a final punctuation of it.

This wine comes in many forms, ranging from a very simple but delicious fresh style that exhibits a nice balance of kick, mature sweetness, and a hint of wood, to a deeply colored aged version that broods with whiffs of caramelized orange and winter spices. Any style makes for a delicious aperitif on its own, simply poured over ice. But it really comes alive when paired with a little fizz and fresh aromatics.

The drink base (all but the ice and tonic) for this can be made in big batches and left in the fridge until needed, then mixed with tonic as called for when ready to serve.

1½ ounces white port (any style will do)

1 sprig fresh mint

1 strip orange zest

Ice cubes

4 ounces tonic water

In a cocktail shaker, mix the port with the mint, orange zest, and a few ice cubes. Cover and shake vigorously two or three times. Pour the entire contents into a rocks glass and pour the tonic over to fill. Serve immediately.

Serves 1

Strawberry and Pimm's Sparkler

Pimm's is a wonderful spirit hailing from the UK that has long been a part of the great cocktail tradition. It is a gin-based drink infused with a secret blend of herbs. It has a rather seductive quality to it, a rusty color, and a tealike scent. It is a remarkably refreshing drink when paired simply with slices of cucumber, fresh mint sprigs, ice, and a splash of soda. It also goes very nicely with fruit, and this recipe can be made with just about any ripe summer fruit; one of my favorites is sliced nectarines. I also like to sub out the soda for Prosecco or Cava, but for a lower-alcohol version, stick with the soda.

8 ripe strawberries or 2 nectarines

1½ teaspoons maple syrup

Leaves from 4 sprigs fresh mint

8 ounces Pimm's No. 1

Ice cubes

12 ounces club soda

Hull the strawberries and cut them into quarters (or halve and pit the nectarines and cut them into ¼-inch-thick slices). Mix the fruit with the maple syrup and mint leaves in a cocktail shaker and let sit for 20 minutes to let the juices flow.

Add the Pimm's and stir once to gently crush some of the fruit. Pour the mixture over ice into rocks glasses and top each with club soda. Serve immediately.

Serves 4

Berry-Cherry Sangria

There is hardly anything more appealing than a playful glass of this classic wine punch. A version for the kiddos can be made by substituting cranberry juice for wine and omitting the brandy.

2 cups white grape juice

One 750-ml bottle red wine such as zinfandel or syrah

8 ounces brandy (I prefer Spanish brandy for this, as it has a mellower tone and usually a reasonable price)

1 orange, zest peeled into strips, then juiced

1 lemon, zest peeled into strips, then juiced

Pinch of kosher salt

Ice cubes

1 cup blueberries

1 cup pitted cherries

In a large pitcher, mix the grape juice, wine, brandy, and citrus zests and juices. Add the salt and mix vigorously to muddle the zests so they release their oils. Let sit in the refrigerator until ready to serve, at least 20 minutes but as long as overnight.

To serve, fill the pitcher with ice and stir. Add the blueberries and cherries to wine or rocks glasses, pour in the sangria, and enjoy!

Serves 4

A Venerable Wine Spritzer

For many people, the wine spritzer has become a beverage of ill repute, conjuring up memories of high-school encounters with Boone's Farm or worse. But I think that wine is a great mixer when paired smartly with other ingredients. Get a good-quality wine, but don't go overboard on a bottle that really should be enjoyed on its own. This recipe can also be made in big batches and served from a pitcher. Simply multiply the quantities by eight to use a full bottle of wine.

3 or 4 ice cubes

3 ounces dry Riesling wine (you can get some very nice bottles for about $9)

1½ ounces dry vermouth (I greatly prefer Dolin brand, but Noilly Prat is also good)

1 ounce club soda

1 sprig fresh basil or tarragon

Put the ice in a rocks glass; add the wine and vermouth. Stir to combine and chill. Add the soda and basil sprig and serve immediately.

Serves 1

Crisp Vegetables with Salsa Verde

My wife and I once sailed from Lisbon to Brazil, stepping ashore in some amazing places along the way: Madeira, the Canary Islands, Cape Verde, and then eventually off to the southwest toward Salvador de Bahia in Brazil. Each island stop allowed for off-the-beaten-path culinary exploration. The flavors were vibrant, the wines funky, the people friendly. One of my favorite meals was one we enjoyed at a roadside shack as we hiked the mountainous terrain of Canarias. We were served two chicken wings (yes, just one each), a bottle of rather musky rosé wine, a plate of bananas, and a giant heaping mound of tiny little potatoes, each the size of a marble. The potatoes had been boiled in seawater, and their skins were coated with a delicious salty mineral crust, their insides fluffy and amazingly potato-flavored. Alongside them was a big bowl of salsa verde, the iconic sauce of this island cuisine. The small size of the potatoes and the lack of a fork meant dipping them into the sauce was a rather messy affair, but this was made more socially acceptable by the second nearly finished bottle of wine. It was a transcendent meal, rooted in a specific moment in time, and one we can never reproduce.

So this recipe is a riff on a special memory, pairing salsa verde with crisp raw vegetables, though this salsa will make friends with just about any food you can think of, so go ahead and experiment a little. Any extra will keep in the fridge for four days.

1 cup fresh cilantro leaves (from about 1 bunch)

2 cups fresh flat-leaf parsley leaves (from about 1 bunch)

4 cloves garlic, peeled

½ cup extra-virgin olive oil

2 tablespoons red wine vinegar

Kosher salt

2 bell peppers (any color will do, but I prefer 1 red and 1 yellow)

1 bunch radishes, each trimmed and cut in half

1 small daikon radish, cut into ¼-inch-thick rounds

Combine the herbs, garlic, olive oil, vinegar, and a pinch of salt in a blender. Purée on high speed until the mixture is smooth and then taste for seasoning, adding more salt if necessary.

Slice the peppers in half, remove the stems and seeds, then cut them into strips. Arrange the pepper strips attractively on a platter with the radishes. Spoon the salsa verde into a small bowl and serve it alongside.

Serves 4

Ember-Roasted Squash Hummus

I first tried this dish when I was looking for an interesting vegan option to put on my menus. While my restaurants were certainly vegetarian/vegan friendly, the focus of the menu was anything but. I wanted to present some options that were more than the usual, but I kept coming back to hummus, because it is so delicious. So I tried a few different ways to make it, and this one was a winner. Any type of thick-skinned autumn squash will do in this recipe. My favorites are kabocha, butternut, Hubbard, and regular old pumpkin. I prefer to serve this with baguette slices, but it's also good with toasted pita bread triangles or carrot and celery sticks.

1 medium autumn squash (2 to 3 pounds)

1 cup tahini (sesame paste; available in most grocery stores)

Juice of 2 lemons

1 clove garlic, grated on a Microplane or very finely minced (optional)

Kosher salt

2 to 3 cups extra-virgin olive oil

Freshly grated nutmeg

Espelette pepper (page 55) or crushed red pepper

1 small baguette, sliced on the bias ½ inch thick

Place the entire squash in the embers of a medium charcoal and wood fire (see page 15) after you have finished cooking another meal, or set up a small charcoal fire, place the squash on the grill grate rack directly above it, and cover the grill. The squash, depending on its size, will cook in 45 minutes to 1½ hours. It is done when the skin is charred and the squash deflates a little with light pressure. Let it cool for 20 minutes.

Cut the squash in half, then scoop out and discard the seeds, being careful not to remove too much of the flesh when you do this. Remove the flesh from the skin—scrape right down to the skin, because that is where all the sweet, awesome smoke flavor is! If some charred flakes get mixed in, that's fine.

Place the flesh in a food processor. Add the tahini, lemon juice, and garlic if using. Purée the mixture until it is relatively smooth but there are still a few chunks. Season with a few pinches of salt and then, with the machine running, add the olive oil in a slow, steady stream through the feed tube. The mixture will begin to change color as the olive oil is incorporated. After you have added about 1 cup of the oil, stop the machine, scrape down the side, and taste the hummus. If you think it needs a little more salt, then go ahead and add it. The mixture should be thick at this point, close to a mayonnaise in texture. Turn the machine back on and add another cup of oil, then taste again. The hummus should have a balanced, sweet-sour-smoky-rich flavor. If it seems not quite right, or too thick, continue to add as much of the remaining oil as you need to get the right consistency.

This is best if it is left to chill for a couple of hours before serving, but it can be served right away. Before presenting it to your guests, check the flavor balance one more time and adjust if necessary with more salt and/or lemon juice.

Spoon the hummus into a large bowl and garnish it with a few gratings of nutmeg using a Microplane or nutmeg grater and a pinch of the pepper. Serve with baguette slices.

Serves 4 to 8

Smoked Mackerel Dip

Mackerel and smoke take to each other like fated lovers in a Shakespeare play. Fatty fish like mackerel (as well as bluefish, salmon, and tuna) are perfect for the rustic, woodsy flavor of a charcoal fire and can be used interchangeably in this recipe.

This dip is kind of a play on brandade, the classic purée of potatoes and salt cod. Simmering the potato with the mackerel infuses it with the fish's flavor. The presence of the potato in the mix allows for absorption of the olive oil and contributes to the dip's final silken texture.

7 ounces hot-smoked mackerel (store-bought brands are usually very good)

1 large russet potato (8 ounces), peeled and cut into 1-inch chunks

Kosher salt

4 ounces cream cheese

½ cup extra-virgin olive oil

Juice of 1 lemon

Crostini (recipe follows)

Flake the smoked mackerel into a small pan; discard the skin. Add the potato chunks and cover with cold water. Season with a pinch of salt and bring to a simmer. Cook until the potato is very soft. Drain and transfer to a bowl.

Mash the mackerel-potato mixture with a whisk and add the cream cheese, olive oil, lemon juice, and a pinch of salt. Whisk vigorously until the mixture is a smooth purée.

Serve at room temperature with crostini.

Serves 4

Crostini

This is a basic recipe with many variations. For the purposes of many dishes in this book, I call for bread to be oiled and grilled over live fire. When served hot, just off the grill, this seemingly benign component can add quite a bit to a dish. Crostini should be a contrast in textures, the outside browned and audibly crisp, the inside moist and yielding to the bite.

Bread, sliced (no thinner than ¼ inch thick, but no thicker than ¾ inch)

Olive oil

Kosher salt

Garlic cloves (optional), cut in half

Slice the bread on a slight bias to maximize the surface area. Generously douse each slice on one side with olive oil and season with salt. Grill directly over the coals until the bread is crackling and toasted crisp. Flip the bread to the far side of the grill and cook for another minute or two.

If desired, when the crostini are piping hot and just off the grill, rub each slice with the cut side of the garlic to impart aroma. Serve immediately.

Makes as much as you need

Grilled Chicken Liver Pâté
with Candied Red Onions

Chicken livers are polarizing: you love them, or you think they are disgusting. Contributing to this, I believe, is the fact that chicken liver is one of the easiest things to screw up, and it often happens. But cooked properly, chicken liver is rich, unctuous, and deeply satisfying. In this pâté, the livers are grilled quickly over a hot fire before being reduced to a smooth purée with butter, then layered with vinegar-spiked red onions.

1 pint chicken livers, rinsed, drained, trimmed of any membranes, and patted dry

Kosher salt

Juice of 1 lemon

½ cup (1 stick) unsalted butter, cut into small cubes and kept chilled

1 small red onion, finely diced

3 tablespoons red wine vinegar

3 tablespoons sugar

Crostini (page 52)

Generously season the livers with salt and place them in a grilling basket or perforated grilling pan. Set the pan directly over the coals of a small charcoal and fruitwood fire (see page 15). If you do not have a grilling basket or pan, they can be grilled directly on the grate; just pay attention to placement so they don't end up falling through and into the fire. Cook until the livers have only a little bit of pink left in their centers, about 3 minutes, depending on the heat of the fire. Gently turn them and continue to cook for another minute over direct heat to finish. Remove them to a bowl and let them sit for a few minutes so the residual heat can finish cooking them all the way through.

Transfer the cooked livers to a food processor. Add the lemon juice and a pinch of salt. Pulse to break up the livers, then turn the machine on and slowly add the butter, cube by cube, through the feed tube, waiting until the previous cube has been incorporated before adding the next. If the purée becomes too thick, you can add a few dashes of cold water to thin it. Regularly stop the machine and scrape down the side to ensure a smooth purée. When all the butter has been added, check the seasoning and adjust with a little more salt if necessary. Spoon the purée into a glass crock or a serving bowl and either close the crock or cover its surface directly with plastic wrap and refrigerate.

Combine the onion, vinegar, and sugar in a small saucepan over medium heat. Stir to mix and let cook at a gentle boil until the liquid has reduced to a thick syrup, like cold maple syrup, 20 to 25 minutes. The onion should retain a slight crunch.

Pour the hot onion mixture over the chicken liver pâté and, using a spoon, distribute it in an even layer; re-cover and return the container to the refrigerator.

Remove the pâté from the refrigerator about an hour before serving to let it lose a little of its chill. Provide a knife for spreading and serve it with hot crostini just off the grill.

Serves 4

Citrus and Chile Marinated Goat Cheese

I am not a huge fan of the cheese plate as a premeal snack when having guests over. Cheese is heavy, fatty, and expensive, but because it is also delicious, people usually eat too much of it, thus spoiling their appetites. My answer is to choose a lighter cheese and to spike it with acid and spices to really wake up the palate. This is one of my favorite combinations, and it pairs well with many wines or a hoppy beer.

4 to 6 ounces fresh goat cheese	Crumble the goat cheese into a medium bowl, then mix it with 1 teaspoon salt and the citrus zest. Shape the cheese loosely into a disk about 1 inch thick. Place it in a serving bowl and sprinkle it with the citrus juice and pepper, then season with a little more salt. Gently press the seasonings into the cheese. Pour the olive oil over the top. Let it sit at room temperature for at least an hour or cover it and put it in the fridge overnight (plan to let it return to room temperature before serving).
Kosher salt	
Finely shredded zest and juice of 1 tangerine or orange	
1 teaspoon ground Espelette pepper (page 55) or crushed red pepper	
2 tablespoons extra-virgin olive oil	
Crostini (page 52)	

Spoon the accumulated juice and oil over the cheese to remoisten it. Serve with crostini hot off the grill.

Serves 4

Bruschetta of Cherry Gold Tomatoes and Anchovy

Of all the different types of tomatoes that have found their way to my cutting board, none has ever captivated me like the Sun Gold cherry tomato. It demands your attention, awakes your palate, and wins your heart—in short, it's the best tomato I have ever tasted.

1 pint cherry tomatoes, preferably Sun Gold	Slice the tomatoes in half. Combine them with the garlic, anchovies with their reserved oil, olive oil, and a pinch of salt in a plastic bowl with a tight-fitting lid. Cover the bowl and shake vigorously.
1 clove garlic, grated on a Microplane or very finely minced	
One 2-ounce can oil-packed anchovies, drained (reserve the oil) and roughly chopped	
1 tablespoon extra-virgin olive oil	Spoon the tomato mixture over the freshly grilled crostini and serve immediately.
Kosher salt	
12 Crostini (page 52)	

Serves 4

Celery with Grill-Roasted Pimiento Cheese

I've taken this Southern staple for a spin on the grill. Smoky roasted peppers and cream cheese paired with the cool textural pop of celery is the perfect way to welcome guests.

1 teaspoon canola or olive oil

1 large red bell pepper

4 ounces cream cheese, at room temperature

Juice of 1 lemon

Kosher salt

8 stalks celery, ends trimmed, cut into 2-inch sections

1 tablespoon capers

Lightly oil the pepper and grill it directly over a medium fire (see page 15) until the skin begins to char and blister. Rotate the pepper until each side is cooked the same way. Remove from the grill and let cool. Gently scrape the skin from the pepper and discard. Tear open the pepper and discard the seeds and stem, reserving as much liquid as possible.

Combine the pepper and its juices with the cream cheese, lemon juice, and a pinch of salt in a food processor, then purée until smooth.

Fill each celery stick with a spoonful of the pepper cheese. Garnish each piece with a couple of capers and serve at room temperature.

Serves 4

INGREDIENTS I LOVE: ESPELETTE PEPPER

The famous pepper of Basque cuisine (also sold as *piment d'Espelette*), the Espelette is a small red pepper that is dried and then powdered to be used in almost any application. It has a heady aroma that is at once sweet, earthy, and complex. The pepper does not pack much kick but does have a flirtatious heat that enlivens the palate. It is a perfect substitute for cayenne or even black pepper if you want a nuanced flavor without the burn.

Deviled Eggs Three Ways

Here are three ways I like to prepare this classic finger food. The key to any deviled egg is the quality of the egg. Buy the freshest farm eggs you can find and get a few more than you think you'll need, because the fresher the eggs, the harder they are to peel, so a few may get mussed in the process. This recipe assumes you will be making all three kinds at the same time, for an assortment. If you want to make just one, triple the ingredients for it.

12 eggs (4 for each recipe), hard-boiled in water with a dash of vinegar, peeled, and chilled

CRAB SALAD STUFFED EGGS:
4 ounces fresh claw or backfin blue crabmeat or Dungeness crabmeat, picked over for cartilage and shells

2 teaspoons Old Bay Seasoning

1 tablespoon mayonnaise

HAM SALAD STUFFED EGGS:
1 teaspoon sweet pickle relish

¼ cup diced ham, such as prosciutto or deli ham

1 tablespoon mayonnaise

SMOKY DEVILED EGGS:
1 teaspoon smoked sweet paprika

1½ tablespoons mayonnaise

1 teaspoon cider vinegar

Kosher salt

FOR GARNISH:
Additional crabmeat

8 small cubes of ham

Smoked sweet paprika

Salad greens

Cut the eggs in half lengthwise and remove the yolks. Evenly divide the yolks among three bowls. Add the ingredients for one type of stuffed eggs to each bowl. Mash the ingredients together with a fork to combine. Taste each for seasoning and adjust if necessary. Spoon each filling into one third of the egg white halves.

According to the type of stuffed egg, garnish each with a bit of crabmeat, a cube of ham, or a sprinkle of smoked paprika. Place the stuffed eggs on a platter decorated with a tuft of greens and serve immediately, or refrigerate them and return them to room temperature before serving.

Makes 18 to 24 stuffed eggs

AN ODE TO THE OYSTER

There is no better way to begin to a meal, and no better way to welcome guests than to provide a luxurious quantity of freshly shucked, ice-cold oysters on the half shell.

Oysters and their nearly infinite range of tastes and textures have inspired many great books that have tried mightily to make sense of this mysterious, shiny, opalescent culinary gem sitting gift-like in its pearly shell.

Much is made in the wine world of *terroir,* a French term for the sum of all factors affecting the taste of a wine—the soil type and its mineral content, the sun, the wind, the rain, all acting in concert. This is equally true of the oyster, and recently some folks have begun using the term *merroir* to describe the factors that combine to determine the experience of eating a particular oyster harvested from a particular area. Each oyster carries in its shell a history of every event it has witnessed—every rainstorm or drought that altered the salinity of the water, every change in tide, every shift in water quality or available food resources. And to a discerning enthusiast, all of this is a very big deal, to the degree that an oyster grown on one bank of a bay or inlet might taste completely different from one plucked from the other shore. On top of this, not only are there habitat variables, but also there are different species of oyster, each with its own unique characteristics. If you'd like to dive deeper into this topic, I suggest you pick up Rowan Jacobsen's excellent book *A Geography of Oysters.*

Something to note here is that the vast majority of oysters we eat are farm raised. Wild oyster populations are not doing very well, the result of overfishing, habitat loss, disease, and pollution. And oysters are a keystone species, among the most vital inhabitants of their native areas. They keep the whole system working, and when they are decimated, the system begins to fall apart. The good news is that farming oysters in these same waters is a good thing, a very good thing. Farmed oysters perform the same functions wild oysters do, and they are generally of the same species. In some cases, the farmed oysters spawn, helping to restore native populations. Farming oysters also helps to create economic opportunity for fishing communities struggling with depleted oceans. So to my mind, eating a farmed oyster is a good thing because every time you do, you encourage that

farmer to plant at least one more oyster, if not many more. In our modern lives, we are bombarded by stories of how we (humanity) have screwed it all up; the earth, the economy, our health. It can be depressing. And that is even more reason to eat oysters. It is one of the few actions we can take that not only does no harm, but also it is something to feel good about, it is an act of restoration, and a delicious one at that.

Oysters beguile with a sensual feminine quality. Aphrodite, the goddess of love, was born of the sea foam, the very essence that oysters and their brine evoke. Casanova and his legendary promiscuity, purportedly fueled by oysters, have given these bivalves a cultish, aphrodisiac status. I am not a scientist, and I do not know of any empirical proof that supports this claim. But I do know that a good meal that includes oysters shared with someone you love, where you look your partner in the eye, talk, and laugh, can be a true invitation to romance.

I think Judy Rodgers, the inspirational chef behind Zuni Café in San Francisco, put it best: "Romance makes oysters better." Amen, sister!

HOW TO SHUCK A RAW OYSTER

1. Using a hand towel to protect the hand that holds the oyster, find the hinge at the narrow end of the oyster and insert the tip of a shucking knife between the two shells.

2. Wiggle the knife until it is firmly lodged between the shells, then twist the whole knife to pry the top and bottom shells apart. Wipe the knife on the towel to remove any mud or shell fragments.

3. Slide the knife along the underside of the top shell to release the meat of the oyster. Be careful to keep all the flavorful liquid.

4. Slide the knife under the bottom of the oyster to release it from the lower shell.

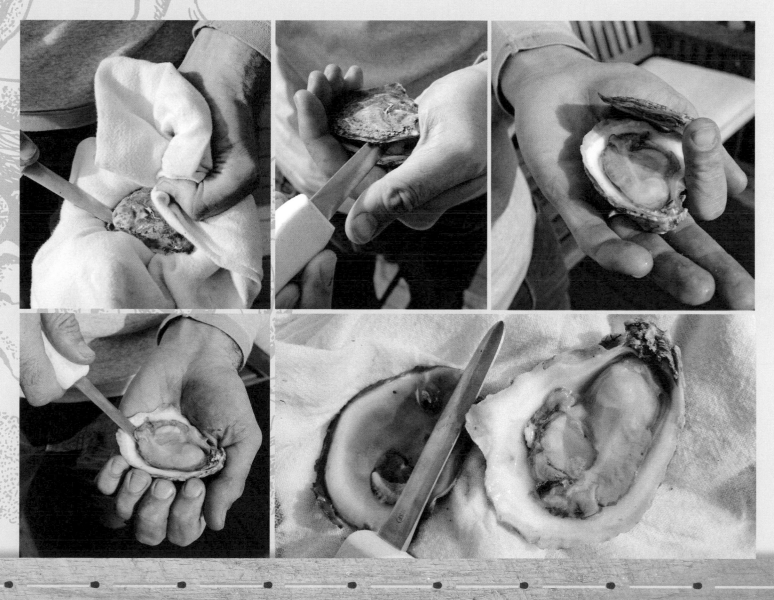

Oyster Sauces

What to put on your raw oysters (if anything) is a very personal decision. To me, it depends on the day, and it depends on the oyster. A super-salty, punch-you-in-the-face-briny Atlantic coast oyster is totally different from a buttery-soft, sweet Gulf Coast oyster. So here is a list of accompaniments, traditional and some not. Take your pick, or choose none at all. But do eat enough oysters to try at least one with each available sauce. When you find the sauce you like best, then open up two dozen more oysters to eat with it!

Lemon wedges The classic. Seafood and lemon are a perfect pair—never competitors, just good friends.

Lime wedges I once heard Rowan Jacobsen, author of *A Geography of Oysters*, say that he prefers fresh-cut limes with oysters. It had never once occurred to me to try limes. Well, I immediately did and found some truth to the man's word. In particular, I feel that lime flatters the greener algal tones of West Coast oysters and can draw out a sweetness in them that is quite charming.

Grilled lemons Giving wedges of lemon (or lime) a pass on the grill infuses them with a hint of smoke and softens their citrus tang by caramelizing some of the sugar content. While this added complexity can be a plus with some oysters, it can sometimes kill the flavor of others such as really minerally tasting West Coast oysters. See page 284 for how to grill lemons.

Cocktail sauce If you're going to use cocktail sauce, make it yourself, mixing together ketchup, prepared horseradish, hot sauce, and lemon juice to your taste. *Do not* use prepared cocktail sauce out of a container— some regional artisanal brands are exempted from this ban.

Prepared horseradish A small dollop on a super-clean-tasting, salty oyster can be quite fun. But I usually only eat one, maybe two of a dozen with just this as a flavor jolt.

Classic mignonette Find a very fresh shallot or small onion. Just before making the sauce, peel and dice it with a very sharp knife so as not to crush it and make it sulfurous. Buy really great-quality red wine vinegar; it should be good enough that you want to take a sip of it. Toast and grind fresh black peppercorns and then judiciously marry these flavors and temper the mix with a few drops of water until you have a perfect balance. Spoon a little bit onto each oyster. Do not save any leftover sauce.

Creative mignonettes Feel free to take liberties with the mignonette. Basically, you are aiming for an infused vinegar mellowed with a little water. Your goal is to make a sauce that suits the personality of the oyster you are serving. On page 61 there are two versions that are a good complement to many of the oysters I like.

Spicy Mezcal Mignonette

3 tablespoons top-quality red wine vinegar

Leaves from 2 sprigs fresh tarragon, chopped

1 celery stick (a stick, not a stalk), diced as finely as possible

Dash of Mezcal Hot Sauce (page 277), or more to your liking

2 to 3 tablespoons water

In a small bowl, mix together the vinegar, tarragon, celery, and hot sauce. Taste it; it will be potent. Add the water 1 tablespoon at a time, tasting as you go until the flavors are balanced. Serve in a ramekin on the side.

Makes about ½ cup

Cilantro–Rice Wine Vinegar Mignonette

2 tablespoons rice vinegar

2 tablespoons Champagne vinegar

Leaves from 4 sprigs fresh cilantro, finely chopped

1 super-fresh shallot or small onion, diced as small as possible

1 teaspoon sugar

1 to 2 tablespoons water

In a small bowl, mix together both vinegars, the cilantro, shallot, and sugar. Taste it; it will be potent. Add the water 1 tablespoon at a time, tasting as you go until the flavors are balanced. Serve in a ramekin on the side.

Makes about ½ cup

Smoked Clams and Mussels

Some people are happy to have a clam shucked before their eyes, then slurp down the briny morsel, the salty liquor of the sea dripping off the shell. But many folks can't understand what all the fuss is about when it comes to the raw bar. This recipe is for them. If you are having a gathering and serving a raw bar, this is a nice way to have a little something for those who prefer their food cooked. The raw aficionados will love these too.

This recipe is really about flavoring the shellfish with smoke rather than preserving them. These will keep for a few days in the fridge, but plan to use them quickly. This recipe is good for any quantity of shellfish, as it is more a technique than a specific list of measured ingredients, so make as few or as many as you want.

1 dozen littleneck clams, scrubbed thoroughly (discard any that won't close)

1 pound mussels (about 24), scrubbed and debearded (discard any that won't close)

2 tablespoons extra-virgin olive oil

1 teaspoon red wine vinegar

Place the clams in a small pot and add an inch of water. Steam them over high heat until the shells begin to pop open. Remove them from the pan as they open and set them aside. When all the clams are cooked, add the mussels to the pot and cook them in the same manner. If any of the shellfish do not open after 8 minutes, discard them.

When all the shellfish are cooked, carefully remove the meat from the shells, making sure to keep them intact. Allow the meats to dry off by placing them on a plate in the refrigerator for about 30 minutes.

Place the meats in a grill basket and set them in a smoker or away from the coals of a small fire in a grill (see page 15). Add wood chunks, preferably alder, oak, or apple, and close the air intake. Cover the grill and smoke the shellfish at low temperature until they have taken on a smoky hue and smell strongly of smoke, about 15 minutes.

Transfer the shellfish to a bowl and coat them with the olive oil and vinegar. Chill them in the refrigerator and keep cold until a half hour before use.

To serve, let the smoked clams and mussels return to room temperature and place a ramekin of toothpicks alongside.

Serves 4 to 6

Grilled Spiced Olives

Olives are underappreciated in this country. I think that we have been culinarily numbed by the canned black olives of pizza fame and the not-so-good green olives that populate cheap cocktail bars. But olives, in all their seemingly infinite varieties, are among the most dynamic and interesting snacks available to start a meal. I particularly like to marinate them with spices and then grill them to accentuate their flavor. In this recipe, I use some of the marinating spices to create smoke that will infuse the olives as they heat through on the grill.

2 cups mixed olives

1 orange, zest removed in large strips using a vegetable peeler, then juiced

1 teaspoon fennel seeds

2 sprigs fresh thyme

1 stick cinnamon

1 tablespoon extra-virgin olive oil

Mix the olives, orange zest and juice, fennel seeds, thyme, and cinnamon together in a medium bowl. Let marinate for at least a day at room temperature.

Remove the cinnamon stick and thyme sprigs (but reserve them) and put the olives in a grill basket. Cook them directly over the coals of a small charcoal and fruitwood fire (see page 15) until they begin to sizzle and caramelize. Move the basket away from the heat, add the cinnamon stick and thyme sprigs to the fire, and cover the grill, letting the smoke infuse the olives with the flavor of the cinnamon and thyme for about 5 minutes.

Transfer the olives to a bowl. Drizzle with the olive oil and serve immediately.

Serves 4

Wood-Grilled Snap Peas with Smoky Aioli

When I was writing *For Cod and Country*, I included a recipe for aioli that I paired with pan-fried potatoes. In testing that recipe, I chose to make the aioli a little creamier by omitting some of the oil. Then, as I had all these batches of aioli around the house after recipe-testing sessions, I would add a little more oil to make it thick and voluminous and use it as a dip for whatever vegetables I had in the fridge, as well on sandwiches and in soups, pink salmon salad . . . just about everything.

Vickie Reh, one of the best chefs in DC and a good friend, serves a similar sauce with grilled young fava beans—the combination is incredible. In this version, I use sugar snap peas, but feel free to grill up almost any kind of vegetable—green beans, asparagus, young carrots, parsnips, whatever looks good at the market— and serve it with a crock of this smoky mayonnaise on the side. *Note:* You might be tempted to toss the snap peas with a little oil before grilling them; don't. If the peas are given even a light coating of oil, the mayonnaise will slip off when you go to dip them. Also, be sure to use farm-fresh eggs for the mayo.

1 pound sugar snap peas, ends trimmed

1 large egg yolk

1 tablespoon smoked sweet paprika

2 tablespoons orange juice

1 teaspoon sherry vinegar

1 clove garlic, peeled

Kosher salt

2 cups canola oil

Place the snap peas in a grill basket and set it directly over the coals of a small charcoal and wood chip fire (see page 15). Grill until they begin to char and soften, 5 to 7 minutes, tossing them as necessary.

Place the egg yolk, paprika, orange juice, vinegar, garlic, and a healthy pinch of salt into a blender. Purée, making sure that the garlic is well incorporated. With the blender running on low speed, gradually add the oil in a steady stream. Do this very slowly at first to make sure that it is being incorporated. As the sauce begins to come together, you can gradually increase the flow of oil, but have patience; if you add it too quickly, the mayonnaise will break. If the sauce becomes too thick, you can add a few drops of cold water to thin it. Once all the oil is added, adjust the seasoning if necessary.

Place the grilled snap peas next to a crock of the aioli and serve immediately. Any leftover aioli can be refrigerated, tightly covered, for up to a week.

Serves 4

Prosciutto-Wrapped Dates

Salty, sweet, fatty, crispy, and rich. Are you sold yet? This easy snack is quick to throw together and a great way to get your guests' appetites roiling. It is a play on bacon-wrapped dates, a cocktail favorite and classic Spanish tapa. Replacing the bacon with prosciutto shortens the cooking time, as well as giving a leaner feel; the hit of smoke flavor is now supplied by a short hop on the grill.

6 to 10 paper-thin slices prosciutto

20 dates, pitted or not (I prefer with the pit, as it prevents gluttony)

Cut each slice of prosciutto across into 3-inch-wide pieces. Place a date on each piece of ham and roll so that it's completely encased.

Grill the wrapped dates just adjacent to the coals of a medium fire (see page 15) you've added apple or other fruitwood chips to. If the prosciutto unrolls, reposition the date so the ham is held in place by the grate. Cover the grill and cook until the prosciutto is crispy, 5 to 7 minutes. Serve immediately.

Makes 20 pieces

Grilled Asparagus with Whipped Ricotta and Pistachio Piccata

I served this as a very elegant appetizer to 400 guests at the inaugural National Geographic Explorers Gala. I had the great honor of creating the entire menu for that evening, and after tossing out many drafts full of rarefied ingredients such as truffles and foie gras, I decided to serve the foods that I like best, including vegetables harvested at their peak and accented with clean, honest flavors.

1 pound asparagus, tough bottoms snapped off

2 tablespoons extra-virgin olive oil

1 cup fresh ricotta cheese

2 tablespoons heavy cream

Kosher salt

1 cup shelled unsalted roasted pistachios

Finely shredded zest of 1 orange

2 cloves garlic, grated on a Microplane or very finely minced

Bring a pot of generously salted water to a boil. Add the asparagus, cook for 1 minute, drain, and lay it on a tray. Drizzle it with 1 tablespoon of the olive oil.

In a medium bowl, mix the ricotta cheese and heavy cream and season with a pinch of salt. Whisk vigorously for a couple of minutes, until the mixture has a smooth, fluffy consistency.

Roughly chop the pistachios and combine them with the orange zest, garlic, and remaining 1 tablespoon olive oil. Season with a pinch of salt and mix well. Let sit at room temperature for at least 20 minutes.

Grill the oiled asparagus directly over a medium charcoal and wood fire (see page 15) until the spears begin to char, about 4 minutes. Remove them from the grill and divide them evenly among the plates. Top the asparagus with a spoonful of the ricotta and then generously scatter the pistachio piccata over each plate. Serve immediately.

Serves 4

Ember-Burnt Leeks
with Smoky Romesco

This classic Catalan dish, prepared here with a slight Americanization, celebrates the beginning of warm weather. Spring onions are grilled over a live fire and served with the iconic sauce of this northern region of Spain, romesco. I love romesco with anything, including fish, vegetables, and simple grilled chicken, and have even used it as a vinaigrette for grain salads. Whenever you make romesco, make a double batch and freeze the extra so you can pull it out in a pinch for an inspired weeknight meal.

For this homespun version, I use leeks, which work wonderfully when roasted directly in the embers of a fire. The tough outer layers burn while the tender insides are permeated with a welcome bittersweet smoke.

2 pounds mature leeks, splayed green leaves trimmed

4 plum tomatoes, each cut into quarters

1 small onion, cut into large dice

1 red bell pepper, seeded and cut into large dice

½ cup slivered almonds

3 cloves garlic, peeled

Kosher salt

¾ cup extra-virgin olive oil

Place the leeks directly in the coals of a medium charcoal and wood fire (see page 15). Scoop the embers to cover the leeks and let them cook until their exteriors are well charred and the flesh is soft to the touch, 15 to 20 minutes. Carefully remove the leeks from the fire and brush off any ashes. Let them cool for a few minutes, then scrape or peel off the burned outer layers.

Combine the tomatoes, onion, bell pepper, almonds, and garlic on a small flameproof tray that will fit on the grill. Season with salt to taste and add 2 tablespoons of the olive oil. Toss to combine and place the tray directly over the fire. Cover the grill and cook until the onion is soft, about 15 minutes.

Transfer the roasted vegetables to a food processor. With the machine running, slowly add the remaining olive oil (½ cup plus 2 tablespoons) through the feed tube in a steady stream. When all the oil is incorporated, check the seasoning and adjust if necessary.

Serve the leeks at room temperature with the romesco in a bowl for dipping.

Serves 4

Grilled Green Beans with Herb Mayonnaise

This is very similar to Wood-Grilled Snap Peas with Smoky Aioli (page 64), but the mayonnaise has a refreshing and much cooler flavor. I tend to like to serve the aioli earlier in the grilling season and this more modest sauce in the midst of summer's heat, when the vegetables are at peak flavor and need only a minor supporting cast to make them shine. Any leftover mayonnaise makes a great base for creamy salad dressings.

½ bunch fresh dill

Leaves from 10 sprigs fresh flat-leaf parsley

½ cup mayonnaise

1 teaspoon cider vinegar

¼ cup extra-virgin olive oil

1 pound green beans, ends trimmed

Kosher salt

The mayonnaise can be made either with a whisk and bowl or in a food processor. If you make it by hand, chop the herbs as finely as possible, combine them with the mayonnaise and vinegar, and mix thoroughly. Slowly add the olive oil to the mixture as you whisk constantly to incorporate it.

If you're using a food processor (which will result in a pleasant-colored sauce), combine the herbs, mayonnaise, and vinegar in the machine and purée. With the machine running, slowly add the olive oil through the feed tube until it is all incorporated.

Place the beans in a grill basket and set them directly over the coals of a medium fire (see page 15) flavored with wood chips; cook until they begin to char and soften, 5 to 7 minutes. Season to taste with salt once cooked.

Serve the beans with a crock of the mayonnaise. Any leftover sauce can be kept in an airtight container for up to a week in the refrigerator.

Serves 4

Grilled Acorn Squash with Charred Pepper-Almond Vinaigrette

Acorn squash is a fabulous vegetable for the grill. The thick skin helps to maintain the structure of the soft, sweet flesh. The skin is perfectly edible, but be sure to scrub it thoroughly to remove any wax. The sweetness of the squash is well balanced by the charred heat of the pepper, but don't go too hot, or the dish will lose its charm.

2 small acorn squash (kabocha, fairy squash, and delicata squash will also work)

Kosher salt

1 tablespoon extra-virgin olive oil

2 Anaheim or Hungarian peppers

3 tablespoons Chunky Almond Oil (page 272)

1 tablespoon white balsamic vinegar or white wine vinegar

8 ounces arugula

Leaves from ½ bunch fresh flat-leaf parsley

Cut each squash in half from top to bottom and scoop out and discard the seeds. Cut the squash into wedges about 1 inch thick, season to taste with salt, and toss with a little of the olive oil. Place the wedges directly over the coals of a medium charcoal and wood fire (see page 15) and cook until they begin to char and caramelize. Rotate the entire grill grate so that the wedges are away from the fire, cover the grill, and let cook for another 10 minutes or so. The wedges should be soft but not falling apart. Remove them from the fire.

Lightly brush the peppers with the remaining olive oil and place them on the grill over direct heat. Cook until the skins are blistered and charred, rotating the peppers until they are cooked in this way all the way around, about 7 minutes. Remove them from the heat and let them sit for a few minutes. Using your hands (wearing gloves if you have them), gently scrape off the charred skins and discard. Slice the peppers in half; remove and discard the seeds and the stem. Dice the peppers and place them into a small bowl. Add the almond oil and vinegar and season to taste with salt. Mix to combine.

To serve, mix the arugula with the parsley and place the greens on a large platter. Lay the squash wedges over the greens, then spoon the vinaigrette over the top. Season to taste with salt and serve immediately.

Serves 4

Grilled Artichokes with Lemony Aioli

I frequently make the two-hour trip between San Francisco and Monterey, California. After dropping down from the winding mountain pass, you drive through the famed agricultural valleys that provided the settings for some of the great American novels of Steinbeck, Saroyan, Stegner, and many others. A few of the tiny farm towns along this route are known for the vegetables they produce; in Gilroy, it's garlic, and in Castroville, it's the artichoke. There is nothing comely, or easy, about an artichoke. It is a food for the dedicated and the patient, but that is a big part of why I like it so; you must slow down, savor each bite. These artichokes are equally good when served with a simple vinaigrette or drawn butter, but the rich and tangy aioli is my favorite.

LEMONY AIOLI:

1 large egg yolk

1 lemon, peel removed in strips, then juiced

1 clove garlic, grated on a Microplane or very finely minced

Leaves from 8 sprigs fresh tarragon, chopped

Kosher salt

2 cups canola oil

GRILLED ARTICHOKES:

4 large artichokes (choose ones with tightly packed leaves and no discoloration)

2 tablespoons extra-virgin olive oil

In a medium bowl, mix the egg yolk, lemon juice, garlic, tarragon, and a pinch of salt. Whisk to combine, then add the canola oil in a slow, steady stream, whisking the entire time. While the temptation is to pour the oil in quickly, patience is the key. If you add it too hastily, the mayonnaise will break and you'll have to toss the whole lot out and start again. The sauce will thicken as you add the oil, until finally it is a smooth mayonnaise. This will keep for up to a week tightly covered in the fridge.

Carefully cut the artichokes in half lengthwise with a serrated bread knife. Let the knife do the work: Slice back and forth rather than exerting heavy pressure, which will likely cause the artichoke to roll and may leave you with a nasty cut. Once they have been cut, scoop out and discard the chokes and the purplish green hairs in the centers. Put the artichokes in a pot and cover them with cold water. Add a generous amount of salt and the lemon peel. Bring to a boil, uncovered, then reduce the heat to a simmer and cook until the thickest part of the artichoke is easily pierced with a knife, 10 to 15 minutes. Strain and let the artichokes rest cut side down to help water drain out from the leaves.

Lightly coat the artichoke halves with the olive oil and grill them directly over the coals of a medium fire (see page 15) infused with maple or oak wood until the edges begin to char.

Serve the artichokes not-too-hot off the grill with the aioli on the side in a small bowl and a large empty bowl to receive the discarded leaves. Oh, and have a lot of napkins nearby.

Serves 4

Crispy Zucchini Cakes with Basil Walnut Pesto

I used to buy quite a bit of produce for my restaurants from a wonderfully fun farmer named Steve Turnich. He ran a little company that would deliver produce from a number of farmers in the Northern Neck of Virginia. It was always a little bit of a gamble. Many of the farmers were Amish, and Steve, I think, would sometimes just guess what was available because, well, he couldn't raise these farmers on the telephone. But his produce was top-notch, and his season was nearly three weeks ahead of the Maryland and Pennsylvania farmers. So Steve was always the bearer of the first asparagus, the first strawberries—you name it, Steve had it first.

Well, one day Steve called me up in an unusually frantic mood. Said something about a big deal going down, mumbling his words. "Gotta get it off my hands", he said over and over. I said "Okay," more out of consolation than any real understanding of what I was agreeing to. The next day, Steve arrived at my restaurant with hundreds of pounds of zucchini. Apparently there had been a bumper crop of this already prolific plant, and . . . now the problem was mine. Zucchini it was. In risotto, grilled, stuffed, sautéed, fried, roasted, so many ways I began to run out of cooking techniques. And then I made these cakes, and the zucchini problem was solved. That is, until I had to call up Steve and beg for more zucchini. They sold well, very well.

2 pounds zucchini, ends trimmed

Kosher salt

2 tablespoons plain Greek-style yogurt or labne

½ cup panko (Japanese-style bread crumbs)

¼ cup extra-virgin olive oil, or more if needed

1 cup Basil Walnut Pesto (page 274)

Shred the zucchini using the largest holes of a box grater, season it generously with salt, and put it into a colander set over a bowl. Let the zucchini sit for at least 4 hours and as long as overnight. You might be a little surprised at how much liquid comes out!

After it has drained, take a small quantity of the zucchini in your hand and squeeze it to extract as much liquid as possible and then place it into a second bowl. Repeat with all the zucchini, then mix in the yogurt and bread crumbs. Toss to combine and let sit for at least 20 minutes so the crumbs have time to absorb any excess liquid. Form the mixture into small patties 2 to 3 inches in diameter.

In a large skillet, preferably a cast-iron pan, heat the olive oil over medium-high heat. When the oil is shimmering, add a few of the zucchini cakes and cook until they are golden brown. Flip the cakes to cook the other side, then remove them from the pan and keep them warm while you cook the remaining cakes, adding more oil to the pan if necessary.

Serve hot with a generous swoosh of the pesto.

Serves 4

Melon with Prosciutto and Herbs

I love the classic Italian pairing of salty-silky prosciutto with tender, aromatic melon. At my local farmers' market, Chef Nathan Anda of Red Apron Butchery sells a variety of charcuterie products that he makes from locally raised animals. It is an amazing treat to have access to these products that are handmade using traditional techniques and also reflect the unique characteristics of the region.

I was walking through the market one day and had just picked up a small muskmelon that was unrelenting in its aroma. I dropped in on Chef Nathan and grabbed a few packs of his sliced prosciutto to make an easy and beautiful dish that was a revelation in its simplicity. The key to this presentation is to have perfect ingredients.

1 melon (cantaloupe, Charentais, and Crenshaw are all good choices, but go for whatever is ripest)

3 ounces prosciutto, sliced super thin

Leaves from 4 sprigs fresh flat-leaf parsley, torn

1 teaspoon crushed red pepper

2 tablespoons extra-virgin olive oil

Peel the melon using a sharp knife and following the contours to remove the skin in small strips. Cut the melon in half and remove the seeds. Slice the melon into sheets no thicker than ⅛ inch thick.

On a large platter, begin to layer slices of melon, alternating with slices of prosciutto, gently turning them into rose-like arrangements. Scatter the parsley and red pepper over the platter, then drizzle with the olive oil. Serve at room temperature.

Serves 4

Homemade Cottage Cheese with Herbs

It's because of cottage cheese that I met Chef Vickie Reh. Her freshly made cottage cheese is so good that I asked for a personal introduction, and we have been friends ever since. She makes the cheese into large, smooth, perfectly seasoned and textured curds that are then dressed with heavy cream and chives. She serves her cheese with a seasonal accompaniment such as cherry tomatoes, roasted peppers, boiled or pickled beets, etc. I also like it simply smeared on crostini (see page 52).

Be sure to use a thermometer when making the cheese. My first few attempts were complete failures. In talking it through with Vickie, it came out that I had not bothered with a thermometer, using my finger instead to gauge temperature. She admonished me, saying, "Cheese making is science—don't make it up." The next time, I used a thermometer, and the results were perfect.

1 gallon skim milk

Kosher salt

1½ cups distilled white vinegar

1 cup heavy cream

1 tablespoon chopped fresh herbs, such as tarragon, chives, parsley, or chervil

1 tablespoon extra-virgin olive oil

In a large nonreactive pot, heat the milk and 2 tablespoons salt to 120 degrees F over low heat. Stir in the vinegar and turn off the burner. Stir gently for 2 minutes, then remove the pot from the burner and let it sit at room temperature for 45 minutes.

Pour the mixture into a colander lined with a clean tea towel (one that you don't mind possibly throwing out) or several layers of cheesecloth. Wash the cheese under cold running water for a minute or two to cool the curds. Gather up the edges of the towel and compress the cheese, squeezing to press out any excess liquid. When the curds are as dry as possible, chop them into pieces about the size of a pea. Mix gently with the heavy cream and check the seasoning. Add a pinch of salt if necessary.

I like to serve this immediately or within a few hours at room temperature, but it can be refrigerated and served within 2 days, although it will dry out a little. Garnish with the chosen herbs and olive oil just before serving.

Makes about 3 cups

Pesto-Marinated Mozzarella

Mozzarella is a remarkable ingredient. Many grocery stores have begun to carry freshly made mozzarella, a revelation compared to the bland experience of the compressed commercially processed version. True "motz," as it is commonly referred to into professional kitchens, is a thing of wonder. Its delicate texture and wonderfully rich flavor make it a favorite of many chefs. And the best preparations are the simplest.

1 pint fresh
mozzarella
(bocconcini are best
for this recipe)

Kosher salt

3 tablespoons
Basil Walnut Pesto
(page 274)

Crostini (page 52)

Drain the mozzarella well and gently pat dry with paper towels. Cut each ball in half and place the pieces into a medium bowl. Season lightly with salt (be careful how much you use, as it will cause the cheese to weep some of its liquid and dilute the pesto). Add the pesto and toss to combine.

Let marinate at room temperature for at least 30 minutes and up to 2 hours before serving with freshly grilled or broiled crostini.

Serves 4

2
SETTING THE STAGE
Soups + Salads

When you finally gather at the table to enjoy a meal, the last thing you want is to be fussing about in the kitchen. Many of these recipes allow for the dish to be prepared hours in advance and need only a toss at the last moment to refresh or dress them. These dishes are clean, with bright flavors that awaken the palate and excite the appetite for the more substantial dishes to come later from the grill.

I love vegetables, and here you will find a number of recipes that showcase the season in good fashion without making too much of a task. Many of these dishes would be excellent as a light lunch on their own or with the addition of a chicken breast lightly seasoned and slowly grilled. A few of these combined, and I would be a happy man at your dinner table.

The key to a great soup or salad is contrast, and, yes, that applies to both. With a soup, you can introduce the crunch of croutons or a garnish of diced vegetables. But textural contrast in soup is hard to achieve and quick to fade—the sog factor. Any textural garnish must be introduced at the very last moment.

Textural balance is very important in salads, so I give a profile of many different salad greens and how to combine them. But the main task is to balance the flavors, in salads and especially in soups. A spike of vinegar, for example, in gazpacho creates a tangy counterpoint to the cool of cucumber.

You will find many components in each of these salads, so mix and match! If something catches your fancy in one salad and then you spot something else in another, by all means toss 'em up. A salad, at its best, should be a collection of your favorite things.

Cucumber and Buttermilk Soup

There is something really fun about sipping a refreshingly cool yet substantial purée of fresh vegetables as the sun sets on a warm evening. Cucumbers are probably best suited to this type of soup, as no matter how they are prepared, their primary characteristic is a chilly disposition. If the peel is particularly thick, then remove half before chopping. Add a little dill and the tang of buttermilk, and this super-easy dish is finished in just a few minutes.

1½ pounds cucumbers, ends trimmed

Juice of 1 lime

½ bunch fresh dill

2 cups buttermilk

Kosher salt

Hot sauce or extra-virgin olive oil (optional)

Roughly chop the cucumbers and place them in a blender. Add the lime juice, dill, buttermilk, and a good pinch of salt. Purée on high speed until the soup is smooth and creamy. Check the seasoning and adjust if necessary. Pour the soup into an airtight container and chill for at least 30 minutes or until ready to serve.

Ladle the soup into bowls and top it with a drizzle of hot sauce or olive oil, depending on your preference. Both are good!

Serves 4

Smoky Gazpacho

Few soups are simpler than this summer classic, but here I make it slightly more complicated by giving the vegetables a quick turn over a smoky fire to lightly flavor them, not cook them. Although I like raw bell peppers on their own or as part of a crudité, I think they can be a bit of a flavor bully in this soup. For that reason, find the sweetest red or yellow bell pepper you can—by no means should you use a green bell pepper for this.

1 pound ripe heirloom tomatoes (look for sweet and juicy varieties like Brandywine or Cherokee Purple), cored and quartered

1 large cucumber, peeled and chopped

1 red or yellow bell pepper, stem and seeds removed

1 onion, cut into 1-inch pieces

1 clove garlic, peeled, or 1 clove Smoke-Roasted Garlic (page 280), squeezed from skin

2 tablespoons extra-virgin olive oil

2 tablespoons sherry vinegar or red wine vinegar

Kosher salt

Lemon-infused olive oil or Basil Oil (page 270; optional)

Place all the vegetables (including the garlic, if raw) on a small flameproof baking sheet and set it on the grill adjacent to the coals of a small fire (see page 15). Add some strong-flavored wood chips such as hickory or maple and cover the grill. Smoke for 3 to 5 minutes to just barely flavor the ingredients.

Place the tomatoes into a blender and use a spoon to lightly crush them to release some of their juices. Purée the tomatoes until smooth. This will provide the liquid necessary to purée the other ingredients. Add the other vegetables along with the olive oil and vinegar, and season generously with salt. Purée until all the vegetables have broken down and the soup has a smooth consistency. You may need to add a little water, depending on the moisture content of the vegetables. If so, do this just a few spoonfuls at a time. Check the seasoning and adjust if necessary.

I am conflicted on chilling this soup, as I think it can numb the flavors, but it does offer a welcome refreshing quality. So go with what you prefer, room temperature or chilled.

Divide the soup among bowls and, if desired, drizzle with lemon-infused oil, basil oil, or more extra-virgin olive oil.

Makes about 2 quarts or 6 to 8 servings

Peach and Ginger Soup

A cold soup is a fresh way to start off a meal with something a little unexpected. These soups tend to be super light in texture and calories but can really enliven the palate and get people excited about what is to come. Peaches are a sweet fruit, but when paired with the gentle spice of ginger and the earthiness of onions, they are transformed into a well-balanced and nuanced soup perfect for late-summer gatherings. I like to serve this in glasses so it can be enjoyed by my guests as they talk and chat while the fire matures and the evening begins.

1½ teaspoons chopped peeled fresh ginger	Heat a sauté pan over medium heat and add the ginger, onion, and olive oil. Cook until the onion is soft and translucent, about 5 minutes.
1 small onion, sliced	
2 tablespoons extra-virgin olive oil	Transfer the onion mixture to a blender and add the halved peaches, a pinch of salt, and 1 cup water. Purée on high speed, adding more water if necessary until you have a perfectly smooth purée. Taste for seasoning and adjust if necessary. Allow the soup to sit for at least 30 minutes before serving so that the flavors have time to get friendly.
4 large ripe peaches, cut in half and pitted	
Kosher salt	
1 to 1½ cups water	
2 tablespoons crème fraîche or sour cream	
2 tablespoons Chunky Almond Oil (page 272)	Divide the soup among cups, top each with ½ tablespoon crème fraîche and ½ tablespoon almond oil, and serve at room temperature.

Serves 4

Roasted Yellow Pepper Soup with Basil Oil

Yellow peppers are among the most visually appealing offerings of summer's bounty. Their sweet, aromatic flesh and vivid color can add a striking component to a meal. This velvet-textured soup is a great way to make the most of these sometimes-expensive beauties. While the recipe calls for the peppers to be scorched over a live fire, the same can be accomplished in a broiler so that this part of the recipe can be prepared ahead of time. However, the soup loses its vibrancy when refrigerated, so try to make it just an hour or two before guests arrive.

5 large yellow bell peppers

2 tablespoons extra-virgin olive oil

1 small onion, sliced

1 tablespoon white balsamic vinegar or white wine vinegar

Kosher salt

3 tablespoons Basil Oil (page 270)

Freshly ground black pepper (optional)

Lightly coat the peppers with some of the olive oil and place them directly over the coals of a medium fire (see page 15). Cover the grill and cook until the skin of the peppers begin to char and blister. Gently turn the peppers to cook the other side, rotating them a couple of times until the whole pepper is charred, about 10 minutes total. Remove the peppers to a bowl, cover them with plastic wrap, and let sit for about 20 minutes.

When the peppers are cool enough to handle, gently scrape away the charred skin and discard it; don't worry about leaving small pieces of skin clinging to the peppers. Gently tear the peppers, removing and discarding the seeds and stems, and place them on a plate. The peppers should be in strips and sitting in a fragrant pool of their own juices. Remove the equivalent of one pepper, cut it into small dice, and reserve it separately.

In a small sauté pan, heat the remaining olive oil over medium heat, then cook the onion until it is soft and translucent, about 5 minutes. Transfer to a blender. Add the vinegar and the roasted peppers with all of their juice. Purée on low speed until you have a paste. Slowly add cold water, about 1 tablespoon at a time, until the purée is the consistency of a thick soup. The amount of water needed varies greatly, depending on the peppers, but figure on maybe ½ to 1 cup. Season with salt to taste and let sit for at least 20 minutes to allow the flavors to combine.

To serve, ladle the room-temperature soup into bowls, generously drizzle it with the basil oil, and sprinkle it with a spoonful of the reserved diced pepper. I like to add a single crack of coarse-ground black pepper, as the slight floral spice of the black pepper and the sweet aroma of the soup create an intriguing tension on the palate.

Serves 4

Beet and Taleggio Panzanella

I love the way beets pair with all sorts of cheese—goat cheese, blue cheese, Parmesan. Beets are cheese-friendly because they have a wonderful balance of sweetness and acidity with a slight, and pleasing, metallic taste. The key to cooking beets is to salt the cooking liquid very generously. Many people think that beets are bland, usually because they've only ever had the canned kind. I say give them another try.

In this recipe, I use slightly funky Taleggio cheese to offset the earthy beet. Taleggio is similar to Brie in that it is a creamy cheese with a tart yet rich taste. While the aroma of this cheese is a little musty, the flavor is decidedly fruity, with a lasting tang that brings the best out in the beets.

1 orange
1 pound red beets, trimmed of roots and stalks
Kosher salt
3 slices pumpernickel bread
Juice of 1 lime
2 teaspoons prepared horseradish
3 tablespoons extra-virgin olive oil
¼ bunch fresh dill, roughly chopped, about 3 tablespoons
4 ounces Taleggio cheese, diced (as best you can—sometimes it's just too soft)

Squeeze the juice from the orange and set aside. Place the orange rinds and the beets into a small pot. Season the beets generously with salt and cover them with cold water. Bring to a boil, then reduce the heat to low and simmer until the beets are tender when pierced with the tip of a knife, about 20 minutes, depending on their size. Drain and, while hot, scrape off the skins using a few layers of paper towels. Cut the peeled beets into 1-inch pieces, then toss them with the orange juice.

Preheat the oven to 350 degrees F. Cut the pumpernickel into small cubes, spread them on a baking sheet, and bake until crisp, about 20 minutes.

In a medium bowl, whisk the lime juice, horseradish, and olive oil until they emulsify.

When you're ready to serve, toss the beets (along with the orange juice) with the vinaigrette, pumpernickel croutons, and dill and arrange them on a platter. Scatter the cheese over the top.

Serves 4

Dandelion Greens with Pepper and Anchovy

Dandelion leaves are a delicious but overlooked green that most people consider a weed. These dart-shaped leaves are bitter, with a wonderful aroma and tang similar to the Italian green, puntarelle. The leaves have a slight chew to them, making them a good choice for warm vinaigrettes, especially a warm bacon dressing.

Dandelion greens are becoming increasingly available in grocery stores, but you may have your own supply. If you are going to pick your own, make sure they have not been sprayed with herbicides. Wash them very thoroughly in cold water mixed with a few drops of bleach before using them.

1 pound dandelion greens

1 small red onion, thinly sliced vertically

3 tablespoons Anchovy Vinaigrette (page 278)

Freshly ground black pepper

2 ounces Parmesan cheese

Kosher salt

Snap off any particularly thick dandelion stems and discard them. Arrange the leaves on a platter and scatter the onion over the top. Drizzle with the vinaigrette, then give it about 5 cracks of coarse-ground pepper.

Shave the Parmesan with a vegetable peeler into paper-thin sheets; lay them over the salad. It may need a little sprinkling of salt, but taste it first; the vinaigrette and Parmesan may provide enough seasoning. Serve immediately.

Serves 4

Crunchy Celery Salad with Parmesan and Creamy Lemon Dressing

Celery is mainly used as an aromatic for stocks, but I have found it can be a compelling ingredient in its own right. The vitality of its crunch, the cool, unyielding flavor, and its generally amiable nature make it a valuable staple to have on hand at all times.

The key to this salad is to slice the celery as thinly as possible, preferably with a mandoline. The dish is delicious just the way it is, but I have also spiked it with thin slices of smoked shrimp and loved it. Smoked mussels, clams, even smoked chicken would make nice additions as well.

1 bunch celery, tough outer stalks discarded and ends trimmed

2 tablespoons roughly chopped or torn fresh flat-leaf parsley

¼ cup chopped pecans

Juice of 1 lemon

2 teaspoons whole-grain mustard

2 teaspoons maple syrup or honey

2 tablespoons extra-virgin olive oil

Kosher salt

Freshly ground black pepper

1 ounce Parmesan, cut into shavings with a vegetable peeler

Slice the celery as thin as possible on a slight bias. Do not discard the inner leaves from the heart of the celery, as these are packed with flavor and aroma. Mix the celery with the parsley and pecans in a medium serving bowl.

Mix the lemon juice, mustard, maple syrup, and olive oil in a small bowl. Season with a pinch of salt and whisk to combine. Pour the vinaigrette over the celery mixture and add another pinch of salt. Toss to combine and divide the salad among plates. Garnish with freshly ground pepper and thin shavings of Parmesan. Serve at room temperature.

Serves 4

Grilled Potato Salad

I was thinking about what I really liked in potato salad one day when I was hungry. I decided it was bacon, but not because it makes potato salad any better—it's just that it provides something to focus on, like little bits of joy.

I began messing around with recipes and came up with this combination, which borrows from several different styles. I like the creaminess of mayo-based recipes, but not the fat, so I replaced it with Greek yogurt. I enjoy the brightness of a German-style vinegar-based dressing, so I boiled the potatoes with vinegar to better infuse the acid throughout. And, as I mentioned, I like bacon, but I wanted this to be vegetarian friendly, so I smoked the potatoes briefly over a hot grill.

But the true key to making exceptional potato salad is the type of potato used. Make sure you choose one with good flavor. My favorites are the creamy new potatoes or fingerlings, as they have a great texture and a nice, earthy sweetness.

1 pound nugget or fingerling potatoes

1 tablespoon red wine vinegar

Kosher salt

1 medium-hot pepper, such as poblano, Anaheim, or wax pepper

1 tablespoon extra-virgin olive oil

½ cup plain Greek-style yogurt

1 bunch scallions, thinly sliced

Place the potatoes in a small pan and barely cover them with water. Add the vinegar and season generously with salt. Bring to a simmer and cook over low heat just until the skins begin to crack, 15 to 20 minutes, depending on the size of the potatoes. Drain and allow the potatoes to air-dry on a tray for a few minutes.

Toss the potatoes and the hot pepper with the olive oil to coat and place directly over the coals of a small fire (see page 15) spiked with wood chips (nearly any kind will do). Cook for about 5 minutes, letting the potatoes sit undisturbed but rotating the pepper to evenly char the skin.

Transfer the potatoes to a serving bowl. Place the pepper on a cutting board. Scrape the skin off and remove the stem and seeds. Chop the pepper finely and add it to the potatoes along with the yogurt and scallions. Add a good pinch of salt and mix to incorporate the yogurt, gently crushing some of the potatoes but taking care not to make mashed potatoes. Serve warm or at room temperature.

Serves 4

Strawberry and Peppery Greens Salad with Crispy Goat Cheese

There are few things as intoxicating as the fragile and flirtatious aroma of farm-fresh strawberries. Where I live, strawberries do not make their appearance until late spring; some years I have to wait until summer. They are truly the first exuberant taste of the season.

I combine that excitement with peppery greens and the creaminess of goat cheese in a beautiful side salad to accompany our first meals outside in the tentatively hospitable nights of spring.

6 ounces fresh goat cheese

Juice and finely shredded zest of 1 orange

Leaves from 1 sprig fresh thyme

Kosher salt

½ cup panko (Japanese-style bread crumbs)

3 tablespoons extra-virgin olive oil

1 teaspoon red wine vinegar

1 pint fresh strawberries, hulled and cut in half

8 ounces peppery greens mix (see pages 88-95 for a discussion on greens)

Leaves from 6 sprigs fresh mint, roughly chopped

Freshly ground black pepper

Divide the goat cheese into 4 equal portions and shape them into disks. Press the orange zest and thyme leaves into one side of the goat cheese disks and season with a little salt. Press the other side of each disk into the panko, using a little pressure to make sure the crumbs adhere.

Heat 1 tablespoon of the olive oil in a small nonstick pan over medium-high heat. Sear the goat cheese on the crumb side until golden brown. Turn the heat off and let the disks sit in the pan until needed. This will help them warm through and cut back on the number of times these fragile croquettes are handled.

Mix the remaining 2 tablespoons olive oil, the orange juice, and vinegar with the strawberries in a bowl. Season with a little salt and allow to sit for a few minutes, until the strawberries begin to release their juices. Add the greens, mint, and a pinch of salt, then gently toss to combine.

Divide the salad among the plates and place one disk of goat cheese, crumb side up, onto each portion. Offer your guests a few cracks of black pepper and serve immediately.

Serves 4

SALAD GREENS

Understanding your ingredients is key to creating the right balance in any salad—bitter, sweet, earthy, floral, crunchy, soft. Each green has its own unique character.

arugula

baby kale

baby mustard greens

Arugula When arugula first hit the scene, it was the lively, peppery new kid on the block. Since its popularity has become widespread, I've noticed that much of the arugula being sold is a lot tamer, perhaps being bred to appeal to a wider audience. Just-picked farm-fresh arugula is still a delight, and some bagged or boxed brands have good flavor—try them and stick with a favorite brand. Look for small leaves with pointy tips and even, green color. The leaves are best when small, about 2 inches, but mature in flavor as they grow, from sweetness to bitterness, at which point they are best cooked. Again, before you use arugula, taste it. If it's in its prime, use it as the bulk of your salad. If it is a little tempestuous, make it a small component of a mixed green salad.

One of my favorite salads is good arugula, thin-shaved sweet apple like Gala or Honeycrisp, and fresh mint leaves dressed with lemon and olive oil.

Baby kale The just-emerged shoots of many different kinds of kale are a delicious addition to a mixed salad. They have a slightly chewy texture and a wonderful earthy flavor. Look for a mix of varieties such as baby red Russian kale, baby lacinato (also known as black, dinosaur, or Tuscan kale), or curly leaf kale. Mix these greens in rather than making them the bulk of a salad. Tender leaves of mature kale can also

be used in salad. Slice them thinly and then give them a generous coating of dressing. Kale is a particularly healthy green, super high in many minerals and vitamins.

Baby mustard greens Just like mature mustard greens, these can pack a punch. On their own, baby mustard greens would be way too overpowering, but a small handful of these lively, tender greens can make a salad memorable.

Belgian endive This lettuce looks more like a dime-store-novel space rocket than a salad green, its obelisk-shaped heads of densely packed leaves resting resolutely on blue wax paper in wooden boxes, the aristocrats of the vegetable aisle. This type of endive is very versatile. I love it for its crisp texture, which is perfect for adding crunch to a salad. It also serves nicely for canapés, each leaf a little canoe-shaped vessel in which to spread goat cheese and orange segments, smoked bluefish pâté—basically anything that can go on crostini can be put into an endive leaf.

When Belgian endive is shredded, it adds great structure to mixed greens. The flavor, while bitter, is by no means selfish or unruly. These leaves, either red or white, are great partnered with arugula, purslane, and mizuna; their flavor also takes well to herbs.

dandelion greens

escarole

Bull's blood micro greens It is a misnomer to call these greens, as they are crimson red, highlighted with shades of midnight. This is a beet green, full of deeply earthy flavor and prone to an iron taste. They do not make good eating on their own, but when paired with other greens such as purslane and herbs like dill and mint, they are among the most attractive and tasty salad greens around.

Dandelion greens What, eat weeds? Yes, eat weeds. Get on the Internet, search Euell Gibbons, and stop spraying Roundup to rid your lawn of this delicious green! See puntarelle, (see page 93), which is culinarily parallel.

Endive frisée or curly endive A member of the chicory family, this is an outlier in the world of mesclun. The ubiquitous bags of soft, tender mixed lettuces that you find at the supermarket have two deviant members, radicchio (see page 94) and frisée. Bleached-green, tree-branch-looking frisée has no place in such company. Leave the soft greens alone. Let the big flavors play by themselves. Frisée is a striking plant, a skeletal thing that (I am about to admit my geekiness) reminds me of the Crystalline Entity that haunted Captain Jean-Luc Picard.

This lettuce is architectural, voluminous, and difficult to dress well. A little bit goes a long way, as it does not wilt under the acid of a vinaigrette, keeping its curved shape. It makes for a stunning presentation but must be paired wisely. Mint, parsley, and dill all bring this bitter lettuce to life. It does well in an equal blending with arugula or mizuna, given a dressing with some sweetness. Frisée is well matched with orange and can stand up to warm vinaigrettes. It is the classic bed upon which venerable French chefs rest a poached egg, scatter bacon lardons, and drizzle Champagne vinaigrette.

Escarole This member of the chicory family is similar to radicchio in flavor but has greater sweetness. It is a broad, leafy green that looks like romaine and shares a similar texture. While characteristically bitter, it has a less acute flavor, thus making it a wonderful mixing green. Try it, especially the tender inner leaves, in a Caesar salad. Escarole also stands alone with great character, especially when balanced by acid/sweet components. It can stand up to hearty flavors, as well as the application of heat; it works well as a braising green.

Fennel fronds While fennel bulb is used in many of the recipes in this book, fennel fronds, the feathery celery-like stalks, are equally fun to play around with. The leaves, which look very much like dill, have an accentuated anise/licorice flavor that is a welcome companion to almost any salad green. Fennel fronds pair particularly well with shredded radicchio, add a playful quality to arugula and mizuna, and bring out a wonderful personality in shaved raw mushrooms dressed with olive oil and lemon. The stalks themselves are often fibrous and not fit for raw consumption. However, they can be used fresh in stocks or left out in the sun to dry and then used as an aromatic smoking fuel (see page 23).

Herbs These aromatic leaves are not just for "herbing" things. Herbs are too often relegated to a finishing role, a confetti to be discharged by overeager chefs. But they can be delightful and deeply satisfying when used as a primary ingredient. Only "soft" herbs like parsley and dill are good when raw, as opposed to "hard" herbs such as thyme and rosemary. Added to a salad, herbs provide a slight distraction, a welcome shift in the expected flavor, a spontaneous and candid reminder to pay attention to the details.

Flat-leaf parsley differs greatly from the curly variety. Curly parsley can be overpowering in flavor and aroma, and I often find the texture to be unpleasantly chewy. Flat-leaf, or Italian, parsley has a more nuanced flavor and an inconspicuous texture when mixed with other greens. I think flat-leaf parsley has a refreshing aroma, similar to the way the air smells just after an early summer rainstorm. That may be too romantic for you, but that is the beauty of herbs in salads.

Dill has a flavor that is altogether cool. Neither assertive nor aggressive, it still sets the tone for everything else. Dill is to food what legendary bass player Paul Chambers was to jazz, working his magic on *Kind of Blue*, then later with the Cannonball Adderley Quintet and others. Sometimes that is what a salad needs, a mellow tone to carry the beat and set the mood. Dill is great mixed with nearly all salad greens. Use it sparingly, though; it works best as an understatement.

dill

Mint is one of the most underappreciated ingredients. A quick glance through this book will show you that I am quite fond of this potent herb. Mint is an accentuating flavor, adding new dimension to everyday foods. Think about a glass of lemonade, then stick a sprig of fresh mint into it. The sweet/sour now has an aromatic/cool component that dramatically alters the character of the beverage. When used to accentuate a dish—or a salad—mint can have intoxicating effects. It is especially good paired with greens like mizuna and arugula. But use good mint. Mint can be very bitter and harsh in its character. Try the leaves before you buy. They should be sweet and light in aroma with no lingering bitterness. Variations of mint such as peppermint, lemon mint, and spearmint are not appropriate for salads. Look instead for Moroccan mint or the variety Kentucky Colonel. I have heard both of these referred to as standard or English mint, but I don't believe those are anything other than local common names.

Indigo frisée This is possibly the most beautiful of all salad greens. It is very similar to endive frisée (see page 91) but distinct enough in appearance to warrant its own paragraph. I sometimes find it to be sweeter and less pungent than its blanched cousin.

Mizuna A very attractive, feathery green with sharply pointed leaves. It has a sweet, floral taste with just a hint of cool spice. If they're just old enough, the stems can have a pleasant crunch. This is a great green for adding bulk to salads, as it is not overpowering and it holds a vinaigrette well.

Puntarelle A member of the chicory family, these dart-like leaves are very similar to dandelion greens. They have a sharp bitterness that can be unappealing to some tastes. I have not often seen it outside of farmers' markets, where the wispy, broad leaves are sold bound at the stalks in bunches. Though its bitterness can be tamed by some rather laborious methods (slicing the stalks razor thin lengthwise on a bias, then soaking it in changes of ice-cold salted water), the best way to enjoy this green is to overpower it. Puntarelle is not to be mixed but eaten alone, either raw and well dressed (a classic Roman preparation pairs it with a robust Anchovy Vinaigrette (see page 278), possibly with sharp aged goat cheese and spicy black olives or grilled over a wood fire and dressed with buttery olive oil.

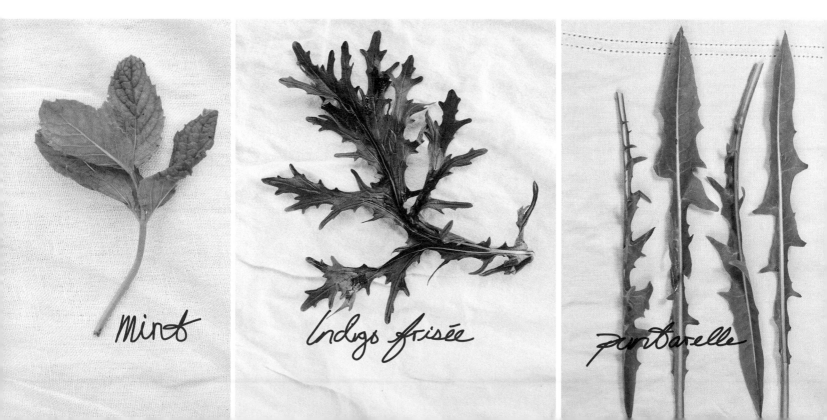

Mint Indigo frisée puntarelle

Purslane Another "newcomer" to the culinary scene—mention purslane at the local garden club, and you may get a few quizzical glances. This "weed" has been haunting gardeners for a long time. It is difficult to kill, and it sprawls everywhere. It also happens to be delicious. This succulent plant has vine-like stalks that snake out low to the ground. The leaves, bright green and clover-shaped, are small and clustered. The stems have a very pleasant crunch with a peppery aroma. The leaves possess an intense lemony scent that really punctuates a salad. It can be served raw, as I prefer, or sautéed in olive oil with shallots. It is a healthful plant that has gained the attention of many nutritionists, farmers, and even the USDA. It also numbers among the few plant-based sources of omega-3 fatty acids.

Purslane can be used alone, garnished with thin-sliced onion and shaved carrots and dressed with a low-acid vinaigrette—think OJ and a lightly flavored olive oil. Or it can be used as part of a mix—try tatsoi, mizuna, and baby kale; be sure to tear the stems into bite-size pieces.

Radicchio This beautiful round, cabbage-like lettuce (though it is actually a member of the chicory family) is a pet peeve of mine, as it's one of the most misused ingredients in America. Though radicchio is bitter, it has a sweet, sly charisma and is crunchy, sometimes even woody in texture. When bought fresh, leaves tightly compact, brightly colored, it can be an inspiring ingredient. But mostly it gets chopped up and thrown into what's sold as "mesclun" mix. It has no place there, not only because its character is wasted in such a mix, but because it ruins the entire salad. Have you ever been set up on a blind date that went horribly wrong, even though the person seemed perfectly nice? Well, that's what happens when radicchio meets mixed greens. Both are totally fine, nice ingredients, just not destined for each other.

Radicchio is hearty, it is bold, it needs some space. When paired with herbs, leaves that by their nature are effusive and giving, and dressed with an anchovy or good citrus dressing, it can be a marvel. But when thrown into a salad for color, it stands out, and not in a nice way. Try making a Caesar salad with grilled radicchio halves, or thinly shred it and pair it with sweet onion and fennel.

Spinach Spinach is usually a cooking green to my taste. But when the leaves are just right and they are well dressed with complementary textures, spinach can be mighty tasty. I have to say that I do not think spinach makes for a good mixing green. Its taste can be too strong for other greens and its dry texture can be a little distracting. Good spinach should be almost crunchy and deeply flavored. The listless "baby spinach" you find in bags and boxes in most grocery stores is not a pleasant ingredient raw. I do, however, enjoy the red-stemmed salad green known as Malabar or Vietnamese spinach. We grew a pot of this on our roof and its vine-like shoots spread across our trellis in beautiful fashion, seeding small red berries between the dark glossy leaves. It was a nice addition to mixed salads, but it was added literally seconds after being picked.

Tatsoi This attractive, dark green leaf has a spoon-like or lily-pad shape and, although it's not assertive, it does have a slight lingering bite, thanks to its mustard family heritage. It is a great blending green.

Watercress This member of the mustard family has good crunch and a cool (think cucumber) pepper kick to it. Often found lining streams and ponds, watercress can be gathered wild in many regions. Be sure to wash it thoroughly in cold water with a few drops of bleach added to kill any possible pathogens (do this with all wild-gathered greens). Cultivated watercress is usually not as intense as its wild counterpart. Watercress makes a wonderful addition to autumn and winter salads, especially when paired with a sweet component like roasted squash or a sweet vinaigrette.

There are many greens and herbs that I have omitted here, some by prejudice, some by ignorance, some because of lack of space. This is by no means a comprehensive list. It is meant to help guide your thinking on how to approach a salad and how to evaluate the offerings at a farmers' market stall. The moral of this short dissertation is to focus on the details. So many amazing flavors are right there, at the same market you already visit, in the same aisles you walk. If you take a closer look, you'll see that it's incredible how much you've been taking for granted but have yet to really discover.

Purslane

Mizuna

Tatsoi

Mixed Citrus Salad

I had a dish like this in a market stall in Marrakech, Morocco, that blew my mind. The citrus was unbelievable. Several kinds of oranges were mixed with mint and an incredibly unctuous, spicy, freshly pressed olive oil. In my interpretation, I have added a few other ingredients, as well as a variety of different citrus fruits. Any citrus will work, so buy what looks best.

1 ruby red grapefruit, peeled, segmented, and each segment cut into 3 pieces

4 clementines, peeled and segmented

1 navel orange, peeled and segmented

Leaves from 6 sprigs fresh mint, thinly sliced

1 small bulb fennel, stalks discarded, thinly sliced

1 small red onion, thinly sliced vertically

¼ cup pitted black olives, such as Kalamata or Niçoise

¼ cup Chile-Infused Oil (page 271) or extra-virgin olive oil

2 or 3 turns freshly ground black pepper

In a large bowl, mix all the ingredients and toss gently to combine. Do not season with salt, as this will draw too much moisture from the citrus, wilting it and making a soup, not a salad. The olives will provide enough seasoning.

Allow the salad to sit for at least 10 minutes and up to a couple of hours at room temperature for the flavors to combine. Serve at room temperature.

Serves 4

Grilled Snap Pea Salad with Onions and Mint

The combination of mint and peas is a culinary gift. This salad relies on the beauty of that pairing, with onion thrown in for a little texture and spice. Grilled snap peas are highly addictive, as a smoky-charred bitterness is matched with their sweet crunch, and who doesn't love smoky-salty-crunchy-sweet-sweet-goodness?

1 pound fresh sugar snap peas

3 tablespoons extra-virgin olive oil

Kosher salt

1 small red onion, thinly sliced vertically

Leaves from 8 sprigs fresh mint, torn

1 tablespoon white balsamic vinegar or red wine vinegar

Toss the peas with a little bit of the olive oil and a pinch of salt. Place them in a grill basket and set it directly over the coals of a small fire (see page 15) spiked with apple wood chips. When the peas begin to char and soften, about 7 minutes, remove the basket from the fire.

Place the peas into a bowl. Add the onion and toss to combine. Let the mixture sit for a minute or two so that the heat of the peas can gently soften the onion. Add the mint, vinegar, and remaining olive oil and season to taste with salt. Toss to combine and serve immediately.

Serves 4

Fennel and Vermouth Raisin Salad with Soft Herbs

Dried fruit is a great snack to have around, but when dried fruits are slowly rehydrated with different flavors, the result is striking. In this case, I use red wine vinegar and vermouth, a fortified wine with a beautiful aroma, to resurrect raisins. The remaining liquid takes on the sweetness and character of the raisins and provides the punch in the vinaigrette.

½ cup raisins of your choice

¼ cup dry vermouth

¼ cup red wine vinegar

¼ cup water

3 tablespoons extra-virgin olive oil

Kosher salt

2 bulbs fennel, stalks cut off

1 small red onion, very thinly sliced vertically

Leaves from 6 sprigs fresh tarragon

Leaves from 6 sprigs fresh flat-leaf parsley

Combine the raisins, vermouth, vinegar, and water in a small pan. Bring to a simmer and cook until the raisins are plumped and the liquid has reduced to a syrup, about 20 minutes. Add the olive oil and season to taste with salt.

Meanwhile, slice the fennel bulb in half from top to bottom and place the fennel flat side down on the cutting board. Slice the bulb crosswise as thinly as you can.

Combine the fennel with the onion and herbs in a medium salad bowl. Add the raisin vinaigrette and toss. The salad is best if it sits for at least 20 minutes at room temperature and can be served up to 2 hours later (do not refrigerate).

Serves 4

Escarole with Nectarines and Ricotta Salata

Most recipes for escarole involve cooking it down for a long period of time over low heat to turn its bitterness into a mellow and sweet flavor. But a good-quality, young head of this lettuce can make for a sublime salad if balanced with a sweet component. In this recipe, it is grilled nectarines, which have a smoky, caramelized sweetness but also maintain some of their piercing acidity. The walnuts add a nice textural component, and the ricotta salata provides a salty punctuation.

Ricotta salata is a salted and pressed version of ricotta cheese. Both fresh goat cheese and feta cheese share its characteristics and can be substituted.

4 nectarines, pitted and cut into quarters

3 tablespoons extra-virgin olive oil

Kosher salt

1 head escarole, trimmed of heavy stems and cut crosswise into 1-inch-wide strips

½ cup chopped walnuts

Juice of 1 orange

1 tablespoon maple syrup (optional)

3 ounces ricotta salata

Freshly ground black pepper

Toss the nectarines with a little of the olive oil and a pinch of salt. Grill the fruit directly over the coals of a small fire (see page 15) until they begin to soften and caramelize, 7 to 10 minutes. Remove from the heat and set aside.

In a large bowl, mix the escarole, walnuts, orange juice, and remaining olive oil. Season to taste with salt and toss to combine. Taste the salad. If it is too bitter for you, add the maple syrup and toss to combine.

Arrange the grilled nectarines around the rim of a platter and place the salad in the middle. Crumble the ricotta over the salad, add a few grinds of black pepper, and serve.

Serves 4

Spicy Cucumber Salad

Cucumbers make one of the most satisfying summer salads. They are everything you want in a vegetable—highly aromatic, cool in flavor, crisp in texture, and they play well with others. Plus they're easy to prep and cheap!

1 large cucumber, peeled lengthwise in stripes

1 small red onion, thinly sliced vertically

1 clove garlic, grated on a Microplane or very finely minced

2 tablespoons salt- or brine-packed capers (if using salt-packed, soak them at least 2 hours in warm water and drain)

Leaves from 2 sprigs fresh mint, thinly sliced

1 tablespoon Chile-Infused Oil (page 271)

Juice of 1 lemon

Kosher salt

Trim the ends off the cucumber, then cut the cucumber in half lengthwise. I like to leave the seeds in, but I know some people prefer them out, so do what you think best. Cut the cucumber across into ¼-inch-thick slices on a slight bias. Combine the cucumber with the remaining ingredients in a medium salad bowl. Toss to combine and let the salad sit at least 10 minutes before checking the seasoning again, as cucumbers have an amazing ability to make salt disappear. Do not refrigerate before serving.

Serves 4

Watercress Salad with Grilled Apples and Ricotta

Watercress is quite possibly my favorite salad green. One summer I was cooking a dinner for 200-plus people in a field in rural Wisconsin. I realized that I did not have enough greens for the salad course that I was responsible for, but earlier I had found a trout pond that was completely covered with cress. I borrowed some waders from one of the workers, and I harvested about twenty pounds of watercress from this small pond. Each stalk, weighted with three leaves, was near perfect in taste— peppery, crunchy, vibrant. My good fortune in finding this bounty made the meal.

In this salad, I contrast the cool flavor of watercress with grilled apples, smoky-sweet and tart, as well as sour-salty ricotta salata.

4 apples (varieties such as Macoun, Winesap, and Honeycrisp are perfect, as they have a wonderful balance of sweet and sour and maintain their crisp texture when grilled), cut into quarters and cored

Kosher salt

2 tablespoons extra-virgin olive oil

1 pound watercress

2 teaspoons red wine vinegar

1 clove garlic, grated on a Microplane or very finely minced

2 teaspoons whole-grain mustard

2 ounces ricotta salata

Season the apples with a pinch of salt and toss them with a little of the olive oil to coat them evenly. Place the apples directly over the coals of a small fire (see page 15) flavored with apple wood and grill until they begin to caramelize and are just tender throughout, about 7 minutes.

In a large bowl, mix the watercress with the vinegar, garlic, mustard, and remaining olive oil. Season with a pinch of salt and toss to combine.

Arrange the dressed greens on a large platter and top with the grilled apples. Crumble the ricotta over the salad and serve immediately.

Serves 4

Summer Corn Salad

Although I prefer to eat my corn straight from the cob, enjoying the satisfaction of removing every kernel from each row, a salad of corn is sometimes more civilized and appropriate for a particular gathering. A salad like this is very simple to throw together and can be made way ahead of dinner; it actually tastes better a couple of hours after being mixed. Keep it out of the fridge, or the corn will become soggy and the flavors numb.

6 ears corn, shucked and boiled for 8 minutes

1 cup cherry tomatoes (Sun Gold is my favorite, though any variety will do; avoid pear tomatoes, as they are mealy and tasteless at best)

1 small red onion, finely diced

2 tablespoons chopped fresh cilantro

Juice of 2 limes

1 tablespoon extra-virgin olive oil

Kosher salt

Cut the kernels from the corn cobs with a paring knife into a large bowl. Do not cut too deeply, or the base of the kernel will be tough—but don't go too shallow either, or you'll lose precious flavor. After the kernels have been cut, scrape the cobs with the back of the knife to "milk" any remaining corn juice into the bowl.

Slice the tomatoes in half and combine them with the corn. Add the onion, cilantro, lime juice, olive oil, and salt to taste; toss to combine. Taste for seasoning and adjust if necessary. Serve at room temperature.

Serves 4

Piquillo Pepper Salad with Goat Cheese and Roasted Garlic

I was introduced to these little peppers on my first day in Spain. I arrived in Madrid early in the morning after a red-eye flight and spent the first few hours wandering around, just taking it all in. I worked up quite an appetite and ducked into a little bar that had caught my eye earlier. I can't remember the name; and on subsequent visits, I have tried to find it again with no luck.

I sidled up to a small bar, the centerpiece of a room that could not have held more than twenty people standing, and enjoyed my first meal in Spain, which convinced me that I had made the right decision in venturing so far from home. The food was simple but well prepared with good ingredients. I have over the years re-created many dishes from this meal, mushrooms with garlic and herbs, salted anchovies with garlic and oil, and so on. This dish is tasty on its own, but for me it is flavored with great memories as well.

Do not be skeptical of the use of canned peppers here. That is about the only way you will find these peppers, and they are of very high quality. The vinaigrette is hard to make in small quantity, so you will have enough left over for another use. It keeps up to a week in the fridge.

1 jar piquillo peppers (about 10 ounces, depending on the brand)

2 ounces fresh goat cheese

Leaves from 3 sprigs fresh flat-leaf parsley, thinly sliced

Leaves from 3 sprigs fresh mint, thinly sliced

Kosher salt

2 cloves Smoke-Roasted Garlic (page 280)

1 tablespoon red wine vinegar

3 tablespoons extra-virgin olive oil

Open and drain the jar of peppers, then gently pat the peppers dry with a clean towel. Cut them in half lengthwise, so that you have two tongue-shaped strips per pepper. Arrange the strips on a large platter and crumble the goat cheese all over. Scatter the herbs and season with a touch of salt.

Combine the garlic, vinegar, and olive oil in a small bowl and mash the garlic cloves until you have a saucy paste. It should be relatively thick and creamy, as the oil will bind with the garlic. Drizzle the vinaigrette over the salad and serve immediately.

Serves 4

Shaved Zucchini Salad

When zucchini is pristinely fresh, it is worthy of eating raw. As it ages off the vine, it begins to lose its moisture and takes on a more leathery chew; it's still fine for sautéing, but do not attempt this dish with anything other than picked-that-day product (a.k.a. farmers' market zucchini). The dark hues of the green skin when shaved make for a very attractive dish, especially in combination with the orange carrots.

2 zucchini (about 1 pound)

2 carrots

Leaves from 6 sprigs fresh mint, thinly sliced

2 tablespoons walnut oil (see page 273)

Juice of 1 orange

2 teaspoons sherry vinegar

Kosher salt

2 ounces Parmesan cheese

Trim the ends off the zucchini and cut each zucchini in half to make two equal cylinders. Using a sharp vegetable peeler, shave the zucchini into thin ribbons, rotating around each section until you reach the seeds. Discard the seeds.

Peel off and discard the outer skin of the carrots, then continue peeling the carrots to make thin ribbons.

Combine the zucchini and carrot ribbons in a medium salad bowl and toss to combine. Add the mint, walnut oil, orange juice, vinegar, and a pinch of salt. Toss to combine and let sit for about 10 minutes.

Use a vegetable peeler to shave the Parmesan over the salad right before serving.

Serves 4

Mixed Heirloom Tomato Salad

The success of this recipe relies solely on the quality of the tomatoes. That's it. What is fun about this salad is that you mix together different varieties, each with its own distinct personality, to make a mélange of flavors, textures, and colors. So play around with different types of heirlooms, and do a little research online to narrow down the field to those whose qualities you are likely to enjoy.

For this mix, I try to always select one crunchy tomato such as a Green Zebra that, even when ripe, still retains a slight bite; a juicy, super-sweet like Cherokee Purple; and a few more acidic types such as Amish Salad or a yellow plum. But ultimately, you should buy what is best at the market and suits your own tastes.

1½ pounds mixed heirloom tomatoes

3 tablespoons Basil Oil (page 270)

Kosher salt (or for a little nuance, use a smoked sea salt)

Cut the tomatoes into bite-size pieces and place them into a bowl. Add the oil and season with salt to taste; very gently toss to combine. The salt will begin to draw out some of the juices from the tomatoes, which will combine with the oil to create a delicious sauce. Give it about 5 minutes and then serve the salad at room temperature. *Never* refrigerate tomato salad!

Serves 4 (generously)

HEIRLOOM VEGETABLES

In nature, plants hedge their bets by evolving a great diversity of genetic variation. This means that the tomato can be found in hundreds of varieties, each with a unique personality. Some are better at dealing with drought, some are cold-hardy, others are high-yielding, and so on. This variety ensures that the tomato, and the farmer, will live on in some form, despite the conditions of nature.

Some of the seeds for these varieties were brought to America by immigrant families who were transplanting to their new world a taste of home. These assembled gifts are the basis of our cuisine. But the melting pot of America took these gifts—the flavors, ingredients, and methods— and eventually boiled this great recipe down to just a few seed varieties most able to conform to mechanized standards.

For this new efficiency, we paid a steep price in the flavor and character of our ingredients. Tomatoes no longer tasted like tomatoes, but they were available in January. Apples came to be defined by a flawless waxy finish and a uniform shape rather than by the joy of eating one. But some folks remembered what these ingredients were supposed to taste like. Some young people believed that there must be something better. Hence the rise of heirloom produce, all due to grandparents who saved a few seeds, garden clubs that sought out challenging varieties, farmers who held flavor in higher esteem than conformity, and universities that studied genetic variations.

Now, many farmers have begun once more to plant these varieties widely and to celebrate the discovery that each taste brings. Chefs have been enthusiastic in welcoming these "new" ingredients onto their menus. Consumers have been discovering the joy of the intriguing range of tastes and textures. Food should be fun and diverse, and again it is. You say something tastes like a squash? Well, which of the hundreds of varieties of squash does it taste like? Tastes like a tomato? Well, is it soft, sweet, and overloaded with summer-sun-warmed juice like a Cherokee Purple, or is it tangy-crunchy and green even when fully ripe like a Zebra?

An heirloom variety is defined in different ways but suffice to say that it is a variety of historical provenance. Eating is not just fueling up, it is an exploration. It can be a coupling of our memories with our present lives. In the taste of an ugly, cracked, misshapen, and odd-colored tomato, you might remember your grandfather in his garden. In the crisp bite of a winesap apple you might find transport to an orchard with its rusty and sultry autumn aura of fermenting fruit.

When filming a TV show in rural Minnesota I met a remarkable group of people who run a farm named Dream of Wild Health. On this farm they offer young Native American families an opportunity to reconnect with the foods of their heritage. Native American children suffer from tragically high rates of diabetes, and in response to this crisis, the farm introduces these children to the glorious, storied, and often heartbreaking history of their culture and cuisine; an understanding of the seasons, almost forgotten grains and vegetables, and the blessing made with the sacred tobacco a prayer for continuity so that the knowledge of elders may be carried forth by the young.

At the end of this visit, I was given an heirloom squash by Sally Auger, the visionary and powerful soul who founded the farm. She quietly gave blessing and revealed to me that the seeds for this squash had been carried by her ancestors along the Trail of Tears. Presenting me with this squash was not just an offering to fill my plate, it was an invitation to participate in the resolute and sorrowful history of a people. But more so, it was an invitation to help celebrate the future of this brave people.

And *that* is an heirloom. A bite of history that transcends accumulated knowledge and defies trends and generational preferences. A simple offering from the past that helps us to better understand and enjoy our time here.

Spinach Salad with Crispy Quinoa and Candied Red Onion Pecan Dressing

Raw spinach can be a little dry on the palate, leaving you with an arid, tannic aftertaste, but I've had some locally grown young, tender leaves that have been revelatory and aromatic, with startling leafy undertones and a whiff of lilies. I tend to like spinach best when briefly grilled or sautéed with red onion and anchovy.

Crispy quinoa is one of my go-to garnishes and an addictive little snack on its own. We usually have a pot of quinoa pilaf in the fridge that we make in big batches and eat throughout the week for breakfast with a little almond milk and maple syrup, as a quick salad with chopped fresh veg for lunch, or as a side dish with dinner. When these nutty little bits are fried in oil, they become the definition of crunch, a welcome and nutritious addition to any dish. You can also bake the quinoa until it is crisp without adding much fat. Just toss in a little oil, spread it on a baking sheet, and cook it at 250 degrees F until crisp, 1 to 2 hours.

¼ cup pecans

¼ cup quinoa

1 small red onion, finely diced

3 tablespoons red wine vinegar

3 tablespoons sugar

Juice of 1 lemon

2 tablespoons extra-virgin olive oil

3 to 5 tablespoons canola oil

12 ounces fresh spinach leaves, trimmed of heavy stems

Kosher salt

Freshly ground black pepper

Toast the pecans on a small baking sheet in a preheated 325-degree F oven for 5 to 8 minutes, and when they have cooled a bit, chop them.

To cook quinoa, wash it thoroughly, then simmer 1 part quinoa to 3 parts lightly salted water until tender, about 20 minutes. Remove from heat and let cool.

Combine the onion, vinegar, and sugar in a small saucepan over medium heat. Stir to mix and let cook at a gentle boil until the liquid has reduced to a thick syrup, 20 to 25 minutes. The onion dice should retain a slight crunch, and the liquid should be thick, like cold maple syrup. Add the pecans, lemon juice, and olive oil and mix well. Let cool to room temperature.

Heat the canola oil over medium-high heat in the smallest skillet you have (the smaller the pan, the less oil you will have to use). When the oil is shimmering and a drop of water sizzles when it hits the surface, carefully add the cooked quinoa and stir to evenly coat it with the oil. Cook until the quinoa starts to turn golden brown and the sizzling sound begins to fade. Test a few pieces by removing them and letting them cool. If they're crunchy, pour the quinoa out of the pan onto paper towels to drain.

Mix the spinach leaves with the onion-pecan dressing and season with salt to taste and a few turns of fresh cracked pepper. Toss to combine, then scatter the quinoa over the salad. Serve immediately.

Serves 4

3 STARS

Vegetables + Accompaniments

I have all too often been let down by the backyard cookout—never by the reunion of friends and family, sometimes by the weather, but usually by the quality of the main dish served. Whether hamburgers, chicken, fish, or whatever, the main dish often requires a forced compliment about the culinary prowess of the host or hostess.

This has taught me to look to the sides for sustenance, and it is where I have found grace. The family heirloom recipe for potato salad, the crisp coleslaw, fresh corn, fragrant fresh fruit, colorful combinations of seasonal vegetables, each given a turn over the coals to accentuate flavor and better reflect the centerpiece of the gathering, the grill.

We tend to think that grilling is for meat and that a cookout is a pagan ritual recalling some masculine ethos of the hunter. Well, what about the gatherer in all of us? A grill is an opportunity to make the cooking method an actual ingredient in your dishes, all of them. To take that wafting scent of smoke, the romantic feel of the outdoor air on the skin, the sense of contentment that comes from a meal set in a different context; all of these are compressed into the warmth of glowing coals, infused into every bite.

To focus a meal so strongly on protein is to deny the vegetables that better reflect the season a place at the table. And it makes a mockery of the fire itself, that it could be so singularly purposed for meat alone.

Throughout this book, you will find that the majority of the recipes are for what we traditionally call the side dishes. But they are given center stage here, because that is where they belong. In these pages you will find a celebration focused on balanced meals that include many textures, flavors, aromas, and ingredients. This is what makes a meal.

Yes, the protein plays a role, it maintains a visceral cultural clutch on our foodways. And this is not ignored, but it is certainly not left to carry the show alone. I have been to that show, and it usually lets me down. It's time to expand the spotlight, to give the supporting cast a chance to steal the scene.

Grilled Asparagus with Spicy Parmesan Sauce

I rarely dress up asparagus; it has such a wonderful flavor that it feels silly to complicate it in any way. But, as the first warm months carry on, cooks and farmers, all eagerly anticipating the next wave of crops, begin to grow a little weary of asparagus. For this dish, I drizzle the grilled spears with a sauce that I made up one day when my wife was desperately hungry and the pickins were slim in the kitchen. We had olive oil, hot sauce, and a little grated Parmesan. I mixed them all together to make a dipping sauce for bread, and she loved it! It is now a staple in our house and plays equally well with just about anything.

Kosher salt

1 pound asparagus, tough stalks snapped off at the base

2½ tablespoons extra-virgin olive oil

1 tablespoon milder hot sauce, such as Tapatío or Frank's Red Hot

1 tablespoon grated Parmesan cheese

Bring a pot of water to a boil and season it generously with salt. Add the asparagus and cook for 1 minute, then drain.

Coat the asparagus with ½ tablespoon of the olive oil and cook the spears on the grill directly over the coals of a medium fire (see page 15) until they begin to char, about 4 minutes. Remove the asparagus to a platter.

Mix the remaining 2 tablespoons olive oil, the hot sauce, and Parmesan and stir to combine. Pour the sauce over the asparagus and serve immediately.

Serves 4

Braised Broccoli with Raisins and Almonds

To the American cook's mind, broccoli exists in a singular spiritless form, the steamed floret, a necessary evil. But it doesn't have to be this way. Broccoli is not only nutritious; it is, in fact, one of the more versatile vegetables we have available to us. It is best when cooked with the addition of liquid at some point in the cooking process in order to soften the fibrous stems, but that is the extent of the rules when it comes to this king of the cruciferian tribe.

This recipe takes its cue from the Italian way with broccoli, and its cousins cauliflower and cabbage, where it is cooked for hours over slow heat. This treatment exiles its sulfurous traits and exposes a beautiful sweetness and depth of character that is a wonder.

This dish is best served at room temperature, which makes it a good choice for entertaining, as the work can be done a day in advance.

1½ pounds broccoli	Cut the broccoli into bite-size florets and slice the stems into ½-inch-thick rounds. If the skin on the stems is particularly thick, peel and discard it before slicing them into rounds.
¼ cup Chunky Almond Oil (page 272)	
1 small onion, cut into small dice	
¼ cup raisins of your choice	Heat the almond oil in a large sauce pot or a sauté pan with a lid over medium heat. Add the onion and cook for a few minutes, until it begins to soften. Add the raisins and broccoli and season lightly with salt. Turn the heat to high and toss to coat the broccoli and raisins with oil. Add the water and bring to a boil. Reduce the heat to low and cover the pan. Cook until the liquid has been reduced to a light glaze, about 1 hour. The broccoli should be very tender but not falling apart. If there is still too much liquid, remove the lid and cook until it is nearly evaporated.
Kosher salt	
1 cup water	

Serve the broccoli immediately, or refrigerate it overnight and let it come back to room temperature before serving.

Serves 4

Grilled Broccoli with Pecan Pesto and Parmesan

Many of us have memories of vegetable mush, perfectly good produce punished in boiling water until it no longer resembled its original form. The tasteless and frankly nutritionally diminished results have been the cause of the never-ending generational dispute that starts with "eat your vegetables," and the knee-jerk response of children everywhere: "no!"

But what if vegetables were crunchy, you know, like French fries? I haven't heard too many stories of parents trying to cajole their children into eating just a few more fries or threatening to withhold dessert if those potato chips are not eaten promptly. We like crispy, we like texture, we like salty. Okay then, let's make broccoli all of those things. Here, the florets, quickly softened in boiling salted water, are then tossed on the grill until they are crunchy, which actually means a little burned. The resulting dish has converted many finicky kids. Add a little fragrant pecan pesto and shavings of Parmesan, and you have quite a beguiling dish for the adults too.

1½ pounds broccoli, cut into large florets, stems reserved for another use

Kosher salt

1 cup pecans, chopped

Finely shredded zest of 1 lemon

1 clove garlic, grated on a Microplane or very finely minced

3 tablespoons extra-virgin olive oil

2 ounces Parmesan cheese, preferably shaved with a vegetable peeler or grated

Bring a large pot of generously salted water to a boil. Add the broccoli and cook for 2 to 3 minutes, then drain and spread the florets on a baking sheet to cool to room temperature.

Toast the pecans on a small baking sheet in a preheated 350-degree F oven for 8 minutes. Transfer them to a small bowl and add the lemon zest, garlic, and 2 tablespoons of the olive oil. Season with a pinch of salt and toss to combine. Reserve at room temperature.

Drizzle the broccoli with the remaining 1 tablespoon olive oil and cook directly over the coals of a medium fire (see page 15) until the florets begin to blacken. Do not move the broccoli pieces during the cooking, just let them sit, let them burn, have faith.

When the florets are nicely colored, after about 10 minutes, remove them to a platter and spoon the pecan pesto over the top. Garnish with a few shavings of Parmesan and serve immediately. This dish is equally good at room temperature; add the pecan pesto as soon as the broccoli comes off the grill to infuse the flavors, but don't add the Parmesan until you are ready to serve.

Serves 4

Grilled Cauliflower with Mint and Parmesan

Cauliflower is a vegetable often overlooked by the creative cook. We tend to think of it as something to steam and serve as is, an oddly bland white specter on an otherwise colorful table. But I have found cauliflower to be one of the most lighthearted ingredients, always willing to give it a go, no matter what the method. So give this underappreciated vegetable a little love. Dress it up, have some fun, let it live a little! I particularly like the combination of the eager flavor of mint and the industrious nature of Parmesan in this simple yet stunning preparation.

1 large head cauliflower

Kosher salt

2 tablespoons extra-virgin olive oil

Leaves from 5 sprigs fresh mint, torn

3 tablespoons Chunky Almond Oil (page 272)

2 ounces Parmesan cheese, preferably shaved with a vegetable peeler, or grated

Place the whole head of cauliflower in a large pot and cover it with cold water. Season generously with salt and place over high heat. Bring to a boil, then turn off the heat and let sit for 5 minutes. Gently remove the cauliflower, set it upside down on kitchen towels, and let it drain fully.

Drizzle the cauliflower with the olive oil and place it floret side down on the grill, directly over the coals of a medium fire (see page 15). Cover the grill and cook until the florets begin to caramelize, about 15 minutes, depending on the intensity of the fire. Do not move the cauliflower, as it will break apart. If you need to adjust the heat, simply rotate the grill grate so that the cauliflower is farther from the fire.

Transfer the cauliflower to a serving platter. Garnish with mint, drizzle with Chunky Almond Oil, and top with Parmesan. Serve the cauliflower immediately as a whole head so that people can easily spoon off sections at the table.

Serves 4

Charred Brussels Sprouts with Orange-Pecan Dressing

The flavors in this dish were inspired by an item that my friend Mike Isabella used to have on his menu when he was chef at Zaytinya restaurant in Washington, DC. He would separate the leaves of the sprouts, deep-fry them until they were shatteringly crisp, then toss them with a coriander-spiked orange vinaigrette. It was a dish that I crave and think of probably once a week. You know a chef is good when the food haunts you for years after.

1 pound Brussels sprouts, stems trimmed, cut in half

Kosher salt

3 tablespoons extra-virgin olive oil

2 tablespoons chopped pecans

2 teaspoons crushed coriander seeds

Finely shredded zest and juice of 1 orange

Add the Brussels sprouts to a pot of generously salted boiling water. Cook until they are tender, about 5 minutes. Drain well and spread on a baking sheet to cool; do not shock them in ice water.

Drizzle the sprouts with 1 tablespoon of the olive oil and toss vigorously to coat. This will help to separate some of the leaves.

Place the sprouts in a grill basket and cook them directly over the coals of a medium fire (see page 15) until they begin to char, then keep cooking them. Yes, burn them, and don't fuss with them too much. Let them burn; that's the secret. When they're well charred, transfer them to a serving dish.

Heat the remaining 2 tablespoons olive oil in a small sauté pan over high heat. Add the pecans and toss to combine. Cook until the nuts begin to toast and release their aroma, about 3 minutes. Add the coriander and cook for another 30 seconds. Add the orange zest and juice and bring to a boil. Season with a pinch of salt, then pour the sauce over the sprouts. This dish is as good served hot as it is at room temperature.

Serves 4

Grilled Corn with Sweet Pepper Butter

Corn and pepper are a great pairing that can take many forms. I like to make salads of roasted corn kernels with diced roasted peppers, both sweet and spicy. But in this case—an ear of corn, grilled till lightly caramelized—it seems wrong to rob you, the eater, of the ultimate joy of corn: the primitive yet socially acceptable summer tradition of simply chowing down! So for this preparation, the pepper is in a flavored butter you can use for slathering.

1 red bell pepper, seeded and cut into quarters

3 tablespoons unsalted butter, at room temperature

Juice of 1 lime

Kosher salt

4 ears fresh corn

Using a Microplane, grate the bell pepper over a medium bowl. Add the butter and lime juice and whisk to combine. Season with a pinch of salt and set aside.

Shuck the corn and steam it or boil it in salted water for 8 minutes. Transfer the corn to the grill, setting the ears directly over the coals of a medium fire (see page 15). Grill until the kernels begin to caramelize. Rotate the ears constantly to cook them evenly.

Remove the corn from the grill and serve it piping hot with the pepper butter on the side.

Serves 4

Corn Pudding

I love savory bread puddings in the late summer, as the nights begin to show the first hint of chill. This recipe makes the most of the sweet corn that floods the farmers' markets at that time of year. It is super simple to make and is best when prepared a day ahead. But don't serve it all to your guests, because leftovers are the best part! The next morning, reheat it in a low oven, top it with a splash of maple syrup, and you have an amazing breakfast.

4 ears fresh sweet corn, shucked

4 large eggs

2 cups milk (whatever type you prefer; this will be rich and luxurious even if you make it with skim milk)

Kosher salt

4 cups bread cubes, cut from a rustic white or farm-style loaf

1 tablespoon unsalted butter

Preheat the oven to 325 degrees F.

Cut the kernels from the corn cobs over a bowl and then, using the back side of the knife, scrape the cobs to release any of the corn juices remaining into the bowl. Put half the kernels into a blender, along with the eggs, milk, and a generous pinch of salt. Purée until smooth. In a large bowl, mix the corn purée with the remaining kernels and add the bread. Mix to combine, gently kneading the bread to slightly crush some of it and form a thick batter. Allow the mixture to sit until all of the liquid is fully absorbed and the bread is soaked through, about 20 minutes.

Grease a 9-inch square baking pan with the butter, leaving any excess butter in small pieces on the bottom of the pan. Pour in the bread mixture, pat it down to evenly distribute, and wrap the pan with aluminum foil. Bake the pudding until it is set throughout and a knife inserted in the center comes out clean, 35 to 40 minutes.

Let it cool slightly so the custard can set. Serve the pudding immediately, or refrigerate it overnight and let it come back to room temperature before you slice it. You can also put slices of pudding on the grill to give them a quick sear just before serving.

Serves 8

Braised Okra with Peanuts and Onions

Okra is one of the few plants that we can successfully grow on our roof. It seems to like the punishing heat of the Mid-Atlantic region, which is magnified by our tar roof. Every day in summer, we have a new handful of tender young okra pods, and they keep collecting, building up in a pile on the kitchen counter. While I am a *big* fan of grilling okra and eating it as a little snack before a meal, we had to come up with other ways to use the excess. Being that okra is a quintessential Southern crop, it made sense to pair it with another iconic regional specialty, the peanut. I find that peanuts tend be dry, but in this recipe they are slowly cooked down, absorbing the flavorful broth as they soften and rehydrate. This dish is equally good when served as a cold leftover, so go ahead and make it a day in advance.

3 tablespoons unsalted butter or olive oil

1 small red onion, thinly sliced

1½ pounds okra, ends trimmed, sliced in half lengthwise

1 cup shelled unsalted peanuts

2 tablespoons cider vinegar

1 cup water

Kosher salt

3 tablespoons chopped fresh flat-leaf parsley

In a large braiser or Dutch oven, heat 2 tablespoons of the butter or all of the olive oil, over high heat until melted. Add the onion and cook for 2 minutes. Add the okra and peanuts and cook for another 5 to 7 minutes, stirring every other minute. Add the vinegar and water. Season to taste with salt and bring to a boil. Reduce the heat to medium low and cook until the liquid is just about evaporated, 10 to 15 minutes.

Remove the pot from the heat and add the remaining 1 tablespoon butter, if using, and the parsley. Toss to combine. Serve the okra immediately, or chill and serve it the next day.

Serves 4

Braised Greens with Bacon and Onion

I have come to love the classic Southern dish of tough field greens braised in an aromatic broth until tender and sweet. There are as many versions of this as there are cooks; and unlike most universal dishes, braised greens, regardless of the prejudices of the cook, are delicious. There are a few things you can do that will really make this dish sing, and the first of these is to use great-tasting greens. The fibrous greens that are typically used for braising—turnip and mustard greens, kale, collards—should be tasted in their raw state before you invest your precious cooking hours in them. A good braising green should be firm to the touch, still animate and turgid. Taste a little sliver of a leaf. Is it overly bitter? Spicy? Does it taste like something you would make a salad of if it weren't for the unending chewiness? The fact that you'll be braising a green is not an excuse to buy poor quality, so shop around a little.

This dish is quite adaptable to the flavors of different greens. If you're using kale, a mild green, follow the recipe as is. If you're using mustard or turnip greens, you might want to be sure to use a sweet Vidalia or Walla Walla onion to balance some of the brisk spice characteristic of those greens. Collards? Consider upping the vinegar to account for the green's relatively earthy, vegetal character.

1 tablespoon extra-virgin olive oil

4 ounces bacon, cut into small dice

1 large onion, thinly sliced

2 pounds braising greens, such as kale, collards, or mustard or turnip greens, stems removed and discarded, leaves torn into bite-size pieces

2 tablespoons cider vinegar

Kosher salt

2 cups water

Heat the olive oil and bacon in a large sauce pot over medium heat. When most of the fat has been rendered from the bacon, about 7 minutes, add the onion. Cook for 2 minutes, then add the greens and toss to combine. Add the vinegar, a generous pinch of salt, and the water. Bring to a simmer, then reduce the heat to low. Stir the greens to ensure that they wilt at an even rate. There should be enough water, especially after the greens begin to exude their liquid, but be sure that the greens are fully covered. Cover the pot and cook for about an hour. Check the leaves for doneness. If they are soft and yield easily to chewing, they are done. If they still need more time, continue to cook them, checking every 20 minutes or so. I know some folks who think that greens cannot be cooked in less than 6 to 8 hours, so experiment away if you wish; it's very hard to take them beyond palatability.

The greens can be served immediately but are best if allowed to chill overnight in the fridge and are reheated just before serving. I like hot sauce with my greens, so offer your guests a bottle of your favorite brand.

Serves 4

Grilled Lacinato Kale

This is simply one of my favorite dishes, and it has a legendary place in the history of my marriage. My wife was not a fan of the vegetable—or of any vegetable. *Fan* might not be the right word. It's not that she just didn't like them; she actively campaigned against them, prosecuting them, all guilty as charged, although on scant evidence.

It was this simple dish that got her to at least begin to consider laying down her sword. The crisp texture, the smoky, charred burn, the transparency of the whole process got her to let her guard down. And now it is a staple. So you might say that this recipe is a gateway vegetable.

Other kale varieties are fine for this, but lacinato is the only variety that crisps rather than wilts, allowing you to get great texture very quickly. This is wonderful with a little Chunky Almond Oil (page 272) drizzled over the top.

2 bunches lacinato kale (also known as black, dinosaur, or Tuscan kale)

2 tablespoons extra-virgin olive oil

Kosher salt

Strip away and discard the stems of the kale. Tear the leaves into large bite-size pieces and toss them with the olive oil and a good pinch of salt.

Cook the leaves briefly over a medium fire (see page 15) seasoned with chunks of maple or oak. They will begin to burn and sizzle almost immediately. This is a good thing. Resist the temptation to turn them; the burn is good; the burn is your friend. After 4 to 5 minutes, turn them once to give a slight char to the wilted leaves that have been on top. Cook for another minute or two, then remove them from the grill. That's it. Serve immediately.

Serves 4

Grilled Bok Choy

I think it's funny that I have eaten bok choy for most of my life, and yet I didn't discover it as an ingredient until a couple of years ago. It is commonly found in steamed or stir-fried vegetable dishes in many Chinese restaurants, but I had never considered using it on its own. It is a highly nutritious food and is so easy to make delicious dishes with. Here I grill it and then dress it simply. This is an easy thing to throw on the grill after the main portion of the meal is cooked and your guests are heading toward the table. It cooks in just a few minutes and possesses a great contrast in textures, as the leaves wilt immediately but the stalks retain a hint of crunch.

1 pound baby bok choy (about 6 heads)

2 tablespoons extra-virgin olive oil

Kosher salt

Juice of 1 lemon

1 ounce Parmesan cheese

Freshly ground black pepper

Cut the bok choy heads in half top to bottom and drizzle the pieces with 1 tablespoon of the olive oil. Place them, cut side down, on the grill directly over the coals of a medium fire (see page 15). Cook until the leaves start to crisp and the stalks begin to soften, 2 to 3 minutes.

Transfer the bok choy to a platter. Season it with a pinch of salt and drizzle with the lemon juice. Shave a little Parmesan over the plate and add a few turns of pepper. Drizzle with the remaining 1 tablespoon olive oil and serve.

Serves 4

Grilled Broccoli Rabe with Walnut Anchovy Dressing and Egg

The warm vinaigrette in this dish is a near perfect partner for any vegetable—roasted root vegetables, sautéed squash, steamed cabbage, you name it. Double the recipe, and it makes a great lunchtime entrée.

1 bunch broccoli rabe (about 1 pound)

Kosher salt

2 tablespoons extra-virgin olive oil

One 2-ounce can oil-packed anchovies

¼ cup walnuts, chopped

Juice of 1 lemon

2 eggs, hard-boiled and peeled, yolks removed for another use (such as eaten with a little salt!)

Trim off and discard about ½ inch from the stem end of the broccoli rabe. Bring a large pot of generously salted water to a boil. Add the broccoli rabe and cook for 7 minutes, then drain it and lay the pieces on a baking sheet to cool to room temperature. Drizzle with 1 tablespoon of the olive oil.

Heat the anchovies and their oil with the remaining 1 tablespoon olive oil in a small sauté pan over medium heat. Gently mash them into the oil with a spatula, then add the walnuts. Cook until the anchovies have melted into the oil and the walnuts are lightly toasted, about 5 minutes. Add the lemon juice and bring to a boil. Remove from the heat and reserve.

Grill the broccoli rabe over the coals of a medium fire (see page 15) until it begins to char, 5 to 8 minutes. Do not turn or otherwise move the rabe until it is done.

Transfer the broccoli rabe to a platter and toss it with the dressing. Grate the egg whites onto the broccoli rabe with a box grater or by pushing them through the holes of a colander. Serve hot off the grill or at room temperature.

Serves 4

Celery Root Slaw

Coleslaw is one of those dishes that endures by tradition rather than by any real sense of devotion to its quality. Now, don't get me wrong, coleslaw can be fantastic, but more often than not, it is a poor excuse for shoveling fat and sugar into your face. And let's be clear on this—I am not talking about your grandma's recipe, I'm talking about everybody else's grandma's recipe.

A good slaw should be crisp in texture and taste clearly of the ingredients it's made with (when is the last time you had slaw that actually tasted like cabbage?). It should be punchy with the acidic tang of vinegar and barely dressed so as to best complement the dish it plays second fiddle to.

This slaw, made with celery root, is equally good prepared with cabbage or carrots. I replace some of the traditional mayonnaise with sour cream, as it contains less fat but delivers the same richness as well as an extra dimension of acid.

Celery root is the better part of the celery family, if you ask me. Its flavor is balanced and sweet, and it has just enough crunch to make it wholly appealing without being singularly textured.

1½ pounds celery root

2 tablespoons sour cream

2 tablespoons mayonnaise

¼ cup cider vinegar

2 tablespoons chopped fresh tarragon

Kosher salt

Use a knife to trim off the brown skin of the celery root. Using a mandoline or the large holes on a box grater, grate the celery root into a medium bowl. Add the sour cream, mayonnaise, vinegar, and tarragon and season with salt to taste; toss well to combine. Let sit for at least 1 hour to allow the flavors to combine; then taste again for seasoning. Adjust if necessary. Serve at room temperature.

Serves 4

Grilled Leeks with Creamy Mustard Vinaigrette

Leeks rarely take center stage in a dish. We add them to soups and stews, fry them for a crispy garnish, or add them to root vegetables for a hearty accompaniment to roasts. But leeks are wonderful in and of themselves. A member of the onion family, they share some of the same pungent characteristics but have a more tempered and balanced flavor. When buying leeks for this preparation, look for young, tender bunches whose splayed leaves are still bright green. The darker growth of the leek is best trimmed off and saved for other uses such as potato and leek soup.

In this dish, the vinegar is added to the leeks while they are simmering, so I'm using the term *vinaigrette* loosely here. The sauce relies on the tang of the leeks to balance the flavors.

1½ pounds leeks, leafy green tops removed and root ends trimmed

2 tablespoons red wine vinegar

Kosher salt

2 teaspoons extra-virgin olive oil

1 large egg yolk

2 teaspoons whole-grain mustard

¼ cup Chunky Almond Oil (page 272)

1 ounce Parmesan cheese

Cut the leeks in half lengthwise, leaving the root ends intact. Wash the leeks under running cold water to remove any sand caught between the layers. Place the leeks in a pan just large enough to hold them and add the vinegar and a generous pinch of salt. Cover with cold water and bring to a boil. Reduce the heat to a simmer and cook until the leeks are tender throughout, 7 to 10 minutes, depending on their size. Drain and let the leeks cool on a baking sheet.

Drizzle the leeks with the olive oil, then set them on the grill, cut side down, directly over the coals of a medium fire (see page 15). Sear just until the edges begin to char, about 5 minutes. Transfer to a platter.

Combine the egg yolk and mustard in a small bowl and add a few drops of water. Whisk to combine, then begin to add the almond oil in a slow, steady stream, whisking as you go. When all the oil has been added, the sauce should have a creamy consistency. Refrigerate it until you are ready to serve.

Spoon the vinaigrette over the leeks and garnish with shavings of Parmesan. This dish is equally good served hot off the grill or at room temperature.

Serves 4

Escalivada

Escalivada is a traditional Catalan preparation of summer vegetables slowly roasted over a smoldering wood fire, then peeled and seasoned. It's pretty much the same selection of vegetables you'd find in a ratatouille or as part of an Italian antipasto platter—and it is a very attractive dish, to boot.

This is a good one to prepare ahead of time and serve at room temperature. The vegetables only taste better after a couple of hours, as they absorb the seasoning and vinegar.

1 large eggplant

1 pound boiler onions (pearl onions will do, but make for more labor)

2 red or yellow bell peppers

2 large ripe tomatoes

3 cloves garlic, peels left on

3 tablespoons extra-virgin olive oil, plus more if desired

1 lemon, cut in half

1 tablespoon sherry vinegar

Kosher salt

Prepare a medium fire (see page 15) in the grill and flavor it with chunks of a fruitwood. Rub the vegetables with 1 tablespoon of the olive oil and place them over the fire in this order: eggplant closest to the fire, but not directly over it; peppers and onions farther out; the garlic and the tomatoes farthest away from the fire. Place the lemon halves, cut side down, directly over the heat and cover the grill. Cook for 10 to 15 minutes, then turn all the vegetables except the tomatoes to ensure that they cook evenly; remove the lemons. Cover the grill and cook until the eggplant is soft and wilting and the onions are beginning to pop out of their skins, about another 20 minutes. Remove everything from the grill and let cool until comfortable to handle.

Cut the eggplant in half, scoop out the flesh in strips, and place them together on a platter. Cut the onions in half, flake the layers apart, discard the skin, and add them to the platter. Scrape the skins from the peppers, cut the flesh into strips, and place them on the platter. Peel and discard the skin from the tomatoes. Cut them into quarters, remove the seeds, cut the flesh into strips, and set them on the platter.

Squeeze the garlic cloves into a small bowl, add the vinegar, the juice of 1 lemon half, and the remaining 2 tablespoons olive oil. Whisk to combine and mash the garlic. Pour the sauce over the vegetables, then season them generously with salt. If you like, drizzle them with a little extra olive oil.

Serve immediately or within a few hours at room temperature with the remaining lemon half.

Serves 4

Ember-Roasted Salt Potatoes with Scallion Cream

The salt potato is a wonder to behold. Those who think that they have experienced the true essence of earthy starchiness that is the potato but have not tried this method are in for a surprise. The secret is to not be afraid of the salt. A true salt potato is boiled in water salted in a ratio of 1 pound salt for every 4 pounds of potatoes. Yes, that is a lot of salt. It's so much salt that it crystallizes on the skins of the cooked potatoes, making them look like something dug up on a paleontological excavation. But, boy, do they taste great.

In this recipe the salt content is reduced and the potatoes are then further subjected to the withering heat and smoke of an aromatic fire. The result? An addictive melding of salty, crunchy, fluffy, flaky goodness.

1½ pounds new potatoes (red or white)

¼ cup kosher salt

½ bunch scallions, trimmed

1 cup sour cream

Place the potatoes in a pan just large enough to hold them and provide a little headroom. Cover them with cold water and add the salt. Cook over medium heat until the potatoes are fork tender, 15 to 20 minutes. Drain the potatoes and let them cool slightly.

Set the potatoes in the embers of a dying fire and cover the grill. Cook until the skins are blistered and the potatoes are heated through, about 20 minutes. Remove them from the coals and brush off any ash. Cut them in half and arrange them on a platter.

Combine the scallions and sour cream with a pinch of salt in a food processor. Purée until the mixture is smooth. Check the seasoning and adjust if necessary, but consider the salt content of the potatoes!

Serve the potatoes either warm or at room temperature with the sour cream sauce.

Serves 4

Grilled Tender Parsnips and Carrots

Many root vegetables sharply spike in sweetness just after the first frost of the season. It's the first signal to the plants to start packing it up, storing away those important sugars for the long winter ahead. Younger carrots, planted toward the end of summer, are still tender and crisp, as are the smaller parsnips, and only produce with these characteristics will work for this recipe. A good way to tell if a carrot or parsnip will be good on the grill is to eat one raw. If it tastes sweet and is more crunchy than chewy, you have a winner.

But you don't have to wait till late in the season to make this, as many grocery stores sell bunches of tender young carrots with their tops year-round.

1 pound tender young carrots, tops trimmed

1 pound tender young parsnips, tops trimmed

2 tablespoons red wine vinegar

Kosher salt

1 tablespoon walnut oil or extra-virgin olive oil

Scrub the vegetables thoroughly under running water, but do not peel them. Place them in a small pot and barely cover them with water. Add the vinegar and season generously with salt. Bring to a simmer and cook until they are just tender when pierced with the tip of a knife, about 5 minutes. Drain and set the vegetables on a baking sheet to cool.

Toss the carrots and parsnips with the walnut or olive oil, then place them on the grill directly over the coals of a small fire (see page 15) flavored with a few chips of fruitwood. Cook for 6 to 8 minutes, rotating them once so they color evenly. Serve them immediately.

Serves 4

Grilled Portobello Mushrooms with Mint Pesto

Portobellos are often served as a meat substitute in vegetarian entrées. But I think that does them a disservice. A portobello, given a delicious marinade and grilled to a smoky char, is oftentimes much better than the insipid mass-market meat it is meant to replace. As a side dish, the grilled caps can be a wonderful addition to a meal, having a texture that is wholly unique and a woodsy aroma that can really excite.

The mint pesto is inspired by nepitella, a wild herb used in Tuscan cuisine. It has a strong flavor that is best described as a cross between mint and oregano. It pairs ridiculously well with mushrooms and in Italy is often given to customers with their purchased mushrooms as a matter of tradition. It can be hard to find here in the United States, but is easy to almost replicate. I omit the oregano in this and use parsley instead to keep the sauce brightly flavored and an attractive green.

4 large portobello mushrooms, stems removed

¼ cup extra-virgin olive oil

Leaves from 3 sprigs fresh thyme

Juice of 1 lemon

Kosher salt

Freshly ground black pepper

½ cup fresh mint leaves (from about 10 sprigs)

½ cup fresh flat-leaf parsley leaves (from about 10 sprigs)

1 clove garlic, peeled

½ cup Chunky Almond Oil (page 272)

2 teaspoons white balsamic vinegar or red wine vinegar

Scrape any dirt off the mushrooms with a knife, but do not wash them. Mix the olive oil with the thyme and lemon juice, stir, and pour the mixture over the ribbed sides of the mushrooms. Season with salt and a few cracks of pepper and let sit for a few minutes, until the salt begins to draw out a little of the mushrooms' moisture.

Place the mushrooms, frilled sides facing up, over a medium fire (see page 15), just adjacent to the coals. Add softly flavored wood chips such as cherry or peach to the fire and cover the grill. Cook for 10 to 15 minutes, rotating the mushrooms clockwise 180 degrees about halfway through so that they cook evenly.

Meanwhile, combine the mint, parsley, garlic, almond oil, and vinegar in a blender with a pinch of salt. Process until the mixture forms a chunky paste and the herb leaves are mostly puréed.

Thinly slice the mushrooms on a bias and arrange them on a platter. Spoon the pesto over the mushrooms and serve them either hot off the grill or at room temperature.

Serves 4

Bacon-Braised Yellow Squash and Tomatoes

I love the vibrant colors of this side dish; if you're not careful, it can actually steal the show. I am not big on putting bacon into dishes just for the sake of bacon, especially in meals centered around the grill, where the smoke flavor is already prominent. But there is something about the smell of bacon and onions sautéing together that elicits a Pavlovian response.

3 ounces bacon, cut into small dice

1 tablespoon extra-virgin olive oil

1 large onion, cut into 1-inch wedges

1 pound yellow summer squash, cut into finger-size wedges

4 plum tomatoes, each cut into 8 pieces

Juice of 1 lemon

Kosher salt

Leaves from 6 sprigs fresh flat-leaf parsley or mint, roughly torn

In a large sauce pot or sauté pan, cook the bacon with the olive oil over medium heat until much of the fat has been rendered from the bacon, about 7 minutes. Add the onion wedges and cook until they begin to soften, about another 5 minutes. Add the squash, toss to coat them in the oil, and cook for 2 minutes. Add the tomatoes and lemon juice and season to taste with salt. Cook until the tomatoes begin to release their juices, then turn the heat to low and cover the pan. Cook until the squash is tender, 15 to 20 minutes.

Remove the pan from the heat. This dish can be served immediately or at room temperature. Just prior to serving, garnish it with the torn herb leaves.

Serves 4

Zucchini with Dried Tomatoes and Mint

This is one of the most satisfying and easy-to-prepare dishes if you have the dried tomatoes on hand. Zucchini is a vegetable that plays very nicely with others. What I love so much about it is that zucchini works with an amazing range of flavors and can express itself differently, depending on how it's cooked and what it's partnered with. In this dish, I tend to slightly undercook the zucchini so that it retains a slight bite and displays a hint of bitterness, which balances well with the sweet/smoky tomatoes.

1½ pounds zucchini, ends trimmed

2 tablespoons oil from Smoke-Dried Tomatoes (page 281)

Kosher salt

3 Smoke-Dried Tomatoes

1 tablespoon red wine vinegar

Leaves from 8 sprigs fresh mint, torn

Cut each zucchini in half lengthwise. Cut each half into 1-inch triangle-shaped chunks. Toss the zucchini with the tomato oil and season it lightly with salt.

Place the zucchini in a grill basket directly over the coals of a small fire (see page 15) flavored with a few wood chips and cook for 5 minutes without moving. Gently toss the zucchini pieces and cook for another 2 minutes, then remove them from the grill.

Slice the dried tomatoes into thin strips. Toss the still-warm zucchini with the tomatoes, vinegar, and mint. Season with a pinch of salt and serve immediately.

Serves 4

Ember-Roasted Squash Purée

I like to make this with heirloom winter squashes; favorites include the red kuri squash, Fairytale pumpkin squash, Hubbard, and Long Island cheese squash. Serve it instead of mashed potatoes for a more colorful table.

1 heirloom winter squash (3 to 4 pounds) such as Fairytale (pictured), red kuri, or Hubbard	Prepare a medium fire (see page 15). When it has burned down to coals, spread them out into a ring and place the whole squash in the center. Add wood chunks of your choice around the squash and let them catch flame. Choke the air intake to just a sliver and cover the grill. The wood will smolder and slowly roast the squash so that the flesh steams in its own juices and becomes lightly scented with smoke. Cook for about 45 minutes to an hour, adding more wood if necessary. The squash is cooked when it begins to deflate and is soft and yielding to the touch. Remove it very carefully from the grill, making sure not to let it fall apart and lose its juice. Let it cool until it's comfortable to handle.
1 tablespoon red wine vinegar	
½ cup (1 stick) unsalted butter	
Kosher salt	

Working on a large tray to catch the juice, cut the squash in half and scoop out and discard the seeds. Scrape the flesh from the skin using a spoon and place it in a bowl. Add any accumulated juice. Add the vinegar, butter, and a good pinch of salt. Mix to combine and mash the squash. The resulting texture should be like that of mashed sweet potatoes. Taste for seasoning and adjust if necessary. Serve hot.

Serves 4

COOKING IN EMBERS

To make the most of the space in your grill, you can place many ingredients directly on or adjacent to the coals of a charcoal fire. This will obviously burn the outside of whatever you are cooking, but the inside will be suffused with a brilliant, sweet undertone of smoke that is different from that of foods cooked above a fire.

You can cook just about anything this way—eggplant, dense winter squash, onions, fish, bread. When I was in Morocco, I spent some time out in the Sahara desert with a couple of Berber tribesmen. When it came time for dinner, a fire of scrub brush was lit and burned to embers. Several types of flour were mixed with water and kneaded. The coals were brushed aside, and the dough was placed in the hot sand where the fire had been. The coals were then scraped back over the dough, and we spent the next hour and a half eating the grasshoppers that were attracted by the light and flew into the fire. The bugs, lightly charred in the embers, were pretty tasty—smoky and crunchy. Then the bread was removed, and our meal was complete.

For me, cooking in embers evokes memories of those desert meals. But even in a decidedly unexotic backyard, it can make magic of the right ingredients.

Grill-Roasted Spaghetti Squash with Molasses and Butter

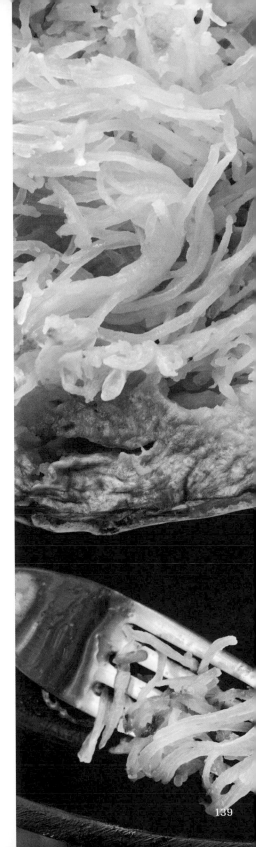

Spaghetti squash is a strange ingredient. In its whole form, it is the most perfect-looking yellow orb, kind of retiring in nature, especially when put next to some of the more unruly kids in the squash family. Even when it is cut in half, it offers no hint as to the provenance of its name. Not until the tender flesh is cooked and the halves are squeezed does the stringy, spaghetti-like texture show itself. Spaghetti squash is very tasty, but with a mild flavor; it lacks the potent sweetness of some other squash varieties. It is best to start it in the oven, then finish it on the grill to ensure that it cooks in the time you expect it to.

1 large spaghetti squash

2 tablespoons unsalted butter

Kosher salt

1½ tablespoons molasses or maple syrup

Preheat the oven to 325 degrees F.

Cut the squash in half lengthwise and scoop out the seeds. Place the squash, cut side down, on a rimmed baking sheet with just enough water to cover the bottom. Transfer the squash carefully to the oven and bake for 25 minutes. Remove it from the oven equally carefully; the water should have evaporated, but you could splash yourself if any remains. Remove the squash from the sheet and allow it to cool at room temperature, cut sides up, until ready to use.

Just before serving, set the squash, cut side down, on the grill directly over the coals of a small wood-infused fire (see page 15). Grill for 3 to 4 minutes, then flip, moving the squash to the coolest part of the grill. Add 1 tablespoon butter to each half, season to taste with salt, and drizzle on the molasses. Cover the grill and cook until the butter is melted, about another 2 minutes.

Take the squash off the grill and, using tongs, squeeze the squash halves to release the flesh. Use a fork to gently shred it and mix it with the butter. Serve immediately in the shells.

Serves 4

Grilled Acorn Squash Wedges

There is a simple beauty in these little sweet-flavored half moons. I love acorn squash cut in half and roasted in an oven, but grilling them gives an added depth. These don't really need a sauce—they eat well as they are—but a drizzle of Chunky Almond Oil (page 272) or Anchovy Vinaigrette (page 278) right before serving can turn them into a very elegant side dish.

2 small acorn squash, seeded and cut into 1- to 2-inch wedges

1 tablespoon extra-virgin olive oil

Grass-Fed Beef Grill Salt (page 265) or kosher salt

Toss the wedges with the oil and season them generously with the salt. Cook them on the grill just adjacent to the coals of a medium fire (see page 15) until they are deeply charred, about 4 minutes per side.

Move the squash as far away from the fire as you can, cover the grill, and cook until they are soft, another 10 minutes or so. Transfer the wedges to a platter and serve immediately.

Serves 4

Grilled Fennel with Anchovy Vinaigrette

While I love the cool crispness of raw fennel, especially when sliced super thin, it takes on a completely different character when briefly passed over a flame. The fire slightly tempers its exuberant crunch and just barely exposes a more nuanced complexity. I like to serve this in place of a traditional coleslaw; in fact, fennel just briefly grilled would be very tasty in place of cabbage in your family slaw recipe!

2 bulbs fennel, stalks discarded and bulbs thinly sliced

1 tablespoon extra-virgin olive oil

Kosher salt

Freshly ground black pepper

1 recipe Anchovy Vinaigrette (page 278)

Toss the sliced fennel with the olive oil and season to taste with salt and 2 or 3 cracks of pepper. Let sit for a few minutes to allow the salt to soften the fennel.

Place the fennel in a grill basket and set it on the grill directly over the coals of a medium fire (see page 15). Placing a few dried fennel stalks on the fire adds a wonderful personality to this dish. Wood chips can overpower the floral taste of the fennel, so if you are using wood, use it sparingly and choose chips or sawdust of delicately flavored woods such as orange, apricot, or alder.

Cook for 5 to 7 minutes without moving the basket so that the fennel on the bottom lightly chars. Remove from the grill and toss to combine. The heat of the fennel on the bottom will help to soften the fennel on top, giving you a range of textures. Toss the fennel with the vinaigrette and serve immediately.

Serves 4

Autumn Caponata

This is a loose interpretation of the classic Italian dish of sweet and sour stewed eggplant. I had something similar when I was filming an episode of a TV show with David Pasternack, the chef at the fabulous NYC eatery Esca, whom I consider to be the best fish cook in America. He and I had spent a day out fishing the waters off Long Island for bluefish and then later prepared a meal for twenty-five or so people at Pasanella and Sons, a small wine shop down by the South Street Seaport. David made a dish like this to complement the rich bluefish, a combination that was simply inspired. The earthy fall vegetables cook slowly together with the last of the summer tomatoes and peppers and become an amazingly harmonious dish. This is best, as most stews are, prepared a day before, chilled, and then reheated before serving.

6 tablespoons Chunky Almond Oil (page 272)

2 stalks celery, cut into 1-inch pieces

1 bulb fennel, stalks discarded, cut into large dice

1 large onion, cut into large dice

1 medium-hot pepper, such as poblano, Anaheim, or Hungarian, seeded and cut into small dice

One 2-ounce can oil-packed anchovies

1 winter squash (about 2 pounds; choose a variety with dense flesh such as kabocha, Hubbard, or butternut), peeled, seeded, and cut into 1-inch chunks

2 large turnips, peeled and cut into 1-inch chunks

2 large ripe tomatoes, cut into 1-inch chunks

2 tablespoons molasses or maple syrup

3 tablespoons red wine vinegar

Juice of 1 lemon

Kosher salt

1 cup water

In a wide, heavy-bottomed stew pot, heat the almond oil over high heat. Add the celery, fennel, onion, and pepper. Sauté for 5 minutes, then add the anchovies with all of their oil. Mash the fillets into the oil until they dissolve. Add the squash and turnips and toss to combine. Reduce the heat to medium and cook for 5 minutes.

Add the tomatoes, molasses, vinegar, and lemon juice and season generously with salt. Stir to combine and cook until the tomatoes begin to break down and release their juices, about 10 minutes.

Add the water, stir to combine, and reduce the heat to low. Cover the pot and cook until the vegetables are soft but not falling apart, about 1 hour. Check the seasoning and adjust if necessary. Cool the stew overnight, then reheat it over low heat before serving it the next day. Or the stew can be served hot off the stove the same day.

Serves 6 to 8

Grilled Summer Vegetables with Green Goddess Dressing

Green Goddess is one of those culinary relics that walks lonely in the cook's creative collective unconscious, just waiting to be plucked from the ether of culinary legacy and given a spot once again on a menu. Once one of the most popular preparations in American gastronomy, it has fallen victim to the generational subjugation of taste preferences, but it is a gem that deserves a more permanent place at our tables. This dressing is equally good with any food, from fish and vegetables both raw and cooked, to chicken and large roasts, so go ahead and make a big batch.

1 cup mayonnaise

One 2-ounce can oil-packed anchovies

Leaves from 8 sprigs fresh tarragon

Leaves from ½ bunch fresh flat-leaf parsley

4 scallions, trimmed and cut into 1-inch pieces

Juice from 1 lemon

1 zucchini or yellow summer squash

1 large onion (I prefer red, but sweet varieties also work well), peeled

1 bulb fennel, stalks discarded

1 small eggplant

3 tablespoons extra-virgin olive oil

Kosher salt

Combine the mayonnaise, anchovies (including their oil), tarragon, parsley, scallions, and lemon juice in a food processor. Purée until the sauce is smooth and has a brilliant green hue. Not all the herbs will break down completely, so there will be some green specks, but this is fine. Allow the sauce to sit in the refrigerator for at least an hour and up to a day for the flavors to marry.

Cut the zucchini into ½-inch-thick slices on a bias. Cut the onion and fennel into 1-inch wedges, keeping the root end intact. Slice the eggplant into ½-inch-thick rounds. Toss all the vegetables with the olive oil and season generously with salt. Let sit for at least 20 minutes to allow the salt to draw out some of the liquid in the vegetables.

Grill the vegetables in batches, starting with the fennel and onion directly over the coals of a medium fire (see page 15) and rotating them after a few minutes to get attractive hash marks. Flip them over and place them on the cooler side of the grill. Repeat the same process with the zucchini and eggplant, in each case cooking until they're just tender.

Transfer the vegetables to a platter and arrange them attractively. Serve immediately, with the dressing in a bowl alongside or drizzled over the top.

Serves 4

Veggie Burger

I have never been a full-fledged vegetarian. There was a week in high school when I suddenly started telling everybody that cows have souls and, therefore, I would not eat them. I still believe that every living thing is sacred, but I started eating meat again and, while I don't eat much of it, it has always been part of the sustenance I am grateful for. I have many vegetarian friends, and I regularly enjoy vegetarian meals. A common misconception of the vegetarian diet is that it's all about finding meat substitutes. As a culture, we tend to stereotype vegetarians as people who make a sacrifice, who are "missing out on something." Not true. Most vegetarians delight in their diet, enjoying the vast array of foods available to them that are not animal-based proteins.

So why, then, do we create all these products that reinforce a protein-centric, center-of-the-plate aesthetic? Tofurky, soy bacon, tempeh "fake meat skewers," and the like. The joy of eating a vegetable-based diet is its diversity, the wide range of tastes and textures and colors that are a nutritionally necessary part of every meal. When I eat a vegetarian meal, I want all of that as part of the experience. I do not want my vegetables and grains puréed and then reformed into a steak-shaped brick. However, I do exempt the veggie burger—actually, this veggie burger, which is my reinvention of the famously delicious one served by the restaurant group formerly known as Houston's. Given a choice between this and an everyday burger, veggie it is, no contest.

2 tablespoons extra-virgin olive oil

1 shallot or small onion, minced

1 clove garlic, grated on a Microplane or very finely minced

2 tablespoons chopped walnuts

2 teaspoons smoked sweet paprika

4 pitted prunes, roughly chopped

1 medium beet, boiled in water to cover until tender, peeled, and shredded on the large holes of a box grater

2 tablespoons red wine vinegar

2 cups cooked brown rice (follow instructions on the package)

One 15-ounce can black beans, drained and briefly rinsed

3 tablespoons oat bran or instant oatmeal

1 large egg (optional)

Kosher salt

4 brioche buns, toasted

Heat 1½ tablespoons of the olive oil in a small skillet over medium heat and cook the shallot and garlic until translucent, about 5 minutes. Add the walnuts and paprika, toss to combine, and cook 1 more minute. Add the prunes, shredded beet, and vinegar. Stir to combine and remove from the heat.

In a large bowl, combine the beet mixture with the rice, beans, oat bran, and egg, if using; season generously with salt. Stir with some force to mash most of the beans and rice into a tacky paste that still has some chunks. Taste for seasoning and adjust if necessary. Chill the mixture for at least an hour.

Form the chilled mixture into four patties, each about 1 inch thick. Brush them with the remaining ½ tablespoon olive oil, then sear them directly over the coals of a medium fire (see page 15) flavored with a few wood chips. When the patties begin to crisp and brown, carefully flip them over and cook for another few minutes.

Rotate the grill grate so the patties are away from the fire, and cover the grill to heat them all the way through, about 5 minutes. Meanwhile, toast the buns over the fire.

Serve the veggie patties on toasted brioche buns. For thoughts about burger toppings see Condiments, page 236.

Makes 4 large burgers

Grilled Garlic Bread

Great garlic bread can be a wonderful complement to a meal. In my version, there is plenty of olive oil and garlic, but I've also added copious amounts of chopped parsley and grated Parmesan for even more flavor.

½ baguette

3 tablespoons extra-virgin olive oil

3 tablespoons chopped fresh flat-leaf parsley (from about 15 sprigs)

4 cloves garlic, grated on a Microplane or very finely minced

2 tablespoons grated Parmesan cheese

Slice the baguette horizontally, as if for a sandwich, and lay the halves crust side down. Mix the olive oil, parsley, and garlic in a small bowl, then slather it over the bread. Let sit for at least 10 minutes for the oil to soak into the bread.

Place the bread, crust side down, on the grill just adjacent to the coals of a medium fire (see page 15). Cover the grill and cook for 5 to 8 minutes to crisp the bread and cook the garlic oil. Sprinkle the Parmesan over the bread, cover the grill again, and cook for another 3 minutes. Serve immediately.

Serves 4

Grilled Pears with Basil Sour Cream

Just underripe pears can be maddening. You buy them with anticipation, carefully selecting them for their comely shape and beautiful color. You make sure there are no bruises and that the stem is intact and was properly snipped, an indication of the care taken with this delicate fruit. You place your pears in a bag, nestled alone or with greens to soften their journey home. With enthusiasm, you set them on the counter in a place of prominence and begin the wait. With determined attention, you watch for any sign that one of them is near ready, hoping to catch it in its fleeting moment of perfection, when the sweetness is tamed by the slight tannic bitterness of the skin, the slight grain in the texture of the juicy flesh like POP ROCKS on your tongue.

The reality is, I have only once or twice caught a pear at its peak. I have come to regard the pear as the ultimate supervillain—beguiling and crafty, it hides its true lunatic nature, its ability to snap, to change faces unnoticed, even while being watched.

So I have stopped trying. Instead I just cook the pears while they are still underripe. Problem solved. And, thus, the inspiration for this recipe. This can either be served as a side dish or as a light and easy grilled dessert.

4 Bosc or Bartlett pears, still firm

1 thumb-size knob fresh ginger, peeled and grated on a Microplane or very finely minced

Juice of 1 lemon

1 tablespoon extra-virgin olive oil

Kosher salt

½ cup sour cream

2 tablespoons Basil Oil (page 270)

Cut the pears into quarters, cut out the cores, and place the pieces in a medium bowl. Add the ginger, lemon juice, olive oil, and a pinch of salt. Toss to coat and let sit for 5 to 10 minutes.

Reserving any marinade remaining in the bowl, grill the pears, cut side down, directly over the coals of a small fire (see page 15) infused with some apple-wood chips until the pears begin to char and the flesh softens, about 5 minutes. At this point, if they need more time to soften, rotate the grate so they are away from the fire, then cover the grill and cook another 5 minutes.

Meanwhile, combine the sour cream, basil oil, and marinade from the pears in a small bowl. Season with a pinch of salt and whisk to combine.

Serve the pears either hot or at room temperature with a dollop of the cream on top of each piece.

Serves 4

4 FINS + SHELLS

Fish + Shellfish

Most who know me understand that seafood is my true passion in life, both at the stove and in the water. I developed this preference when I was very young, as the deft confidence of my father's cooking exposed me to the myriad tastes and textures gifted us by the sea. As a young cook, I sought to learn all that I could about this ingredient, be it a winsome oyster, the mighty salmon, or some unidentified whitefish. It was this focus on ingredients that narrowed the scope of my cooking from being an expression of myself to thinking of the cook as simply a conduit; buy it right, heat it up, serve it with pride.

As ingredients go, there is little in our food world more complicated than seafood and how it gets to our plates. It is a globalized trade that has fed billions, employed millions, enriched thousands, yet impoverished our oceans. We have eaten too many of the fish in the sea, and now we face some great responsibilities. And yet even as we consider the diminishing capacity of the oceans, we are told to eat more seafood for its health benefits.

While these dual responsibilities are seemingly at odds, the health of our bodies and of our oceans are in fact linked, not as opposites but as opportunities. The choices we make at the seafood counter have both very near and far-reaching impacts.

When you buy seafood, buy with courage. Be willing to try something that you have not had before, be willing to ask "what is best today?" This will send you home with the best ingredient, and it will also enable the store, supplier, fishermen to act in concert with the seas and not to force our recipes upon it. When we buy with a preconceived notion of what will be available, what our recipe requires is what we demand of the ocean. Well, the ocean doesn't quite work like that. When a net is cast, a whole host of piscatorial choices is gathered for our tables. If we were willing to eat as the sea affords, then we would be acting as a part of the ecosystem and not as the sovereign consumer of it.

When we eat seafood, we should consume less of it (at each meal), but more of it overall. Small portions are the key to sustainability, nearly across the board. The USDA suggests we eat seafood two to three times per week. This is very easy to do in a responsible way.

When we cook seafood, it should be with as little interference as possible. Your only mission is to apply some heat and stay out of the way. Rarely can we actually improve on the quality of a great piece of seafood. On the grill we can introduce smoke and sizzle, seasonings, and inspired flavors. But still the purpose of the cook is to highlight the ingredient.

As you look through these recipes, do so with an open mind. I have included a few species that might not be in your current repertoire, as well as some old favorites. When you get to the seafood counter, be willing to make substitutions. Also, as you make your decisions, you can look to a number of resources to get an idea of the environmental impact of your dish-to-come. Please see the Suggested Reading section on page 294 for links to websites that will have current information. But most of all, whatever you choose to eat from the sea, eat it with reverence and joy—joy that you may continue to take part in the bounty of the seas.

Fish + Shellfish Grilling Chart

There are hundreds of varieties of seafood to be found at market. However, many people are not familiar with species outside of the charismatic few that take top billing on menus and at fish counters everywhere. This chart helps to make sense of some of the delicious and sometimes sustainable (sometimes not!) options that you may be inspired to pick up next time you shop for dinner. While the list is by no means exhaustive in its scope, I do hope that it inspires you with the confidence to try something new.

While there is no substituting for pristine-quality seafood, there are ways to give your purchases a little extra perk. I prefer to brine nearly every piece of seafood that I cook (tuna being the one exception). It helps to retain moisture and season the fillet evenly throughout. See page 263 for more information.

Amberjack

This fish has continued to grow in popularity with chefs and retailers alike. It has traditionally been a prized sport fish in the Gulf of Mexico. It has the meatiness of steak-like swordfish and the snowy, flaky richness of grouper.

Tip: Amberjack does very well on the grill but must be cooked slowly because of its dense flesh. Smoke should be used minimally, and only lightly flavored smoke at that. The flavor of wood smoke can draw out a metallic/mineral quality that is not flattering.

Arctic char

Chef Rick Moonen calls this "salmon lite," and accurately so. It is a member of the salmon/trout family and shares its characteristic flavors and the orange-pink flesh of salmon. This is mostly a farmed species when found at market and is an excellent stand-in for farmed Atlantic salmon. It is one of the few fish I like to serve with the skin on, as it crisps nicely and adds a clean flavor.

Tip: The flesh of Arctic char is quite fatty and pairs well with maple, oak, and fruitwood smoke. I give the fish a quick sear directly over the coals, then rotate the grate to move it away from the fire. Cook it skin side down with the grill covered to slowly roast the fish and make the most of its sweet flavor.

Atlantic herring

Oftentimes these are sold as sardines, at least those that make it to market; much of the catch is destined for use as bait in the lobster fishery. Oh, how well we feed the little lobsters! The full-flavored fillets flake easily from the bone when cooked. Herring pairs nicely with acidic sauces and grilled citrus.

Tip: Herring is delicious on the grill. Gently scale the fish under running water with a spoon, then remove the intestines and wash thoroughly. Give them a quick brine, then cook over a brisk fire flavored with maple or a fruitwood. Herring takes well to smoking and is also great in pickled preparations.

Barramundi

This thin-filleted fish is a wonderful-tasting product farmed in western Massachusetts and in Vietnam by a company called Australis. It has a sweet, clean flavor and is a widely available substitute for snapper or bass.

Tip: While barramundi is a little difficult to grill, it is worth the effort. It has a thin skin that is prone to sticking and so must be lightly oiled and cooked slowly. It is best grilled with minimal smoke from a lightly flavored wood, as a stronger aroma can hide the sweet flavor of the flesh.

Bluefish

The mighty bluefish is a favorite among anglers, prized for its fierce fight, but not so much for its tasty bite. Oftentimes this fish is dismissed as being oily, a claim that it rightly owns. This fatty quality causes it to go bad faster than most fish, so super-fresh quality is a must with blues. But when they are good, they are some of the best-tasting fish in the sea. Look for smaller fillets, as these have a milder flavor and lower toxicity, which can be an issue with the larger fish.

Tip: When grilling blues, I like to roast them slowly over a smoky fire and serve them with something acidic to mellow out the richness. I remove the skin after cooking, as well as the darkly colored tissue directly beneath it. This is very tasty meat, but it is where toxins can build up.

Catfish

Catfish is one of the most commonly farmed species. There are some issues with the methods of farming, both for reasons of environment and flavor, and your best bet is to look for domestically produced fish. Catfish always benefits from a dunk in a marinade with a little acidity; this can tame the sometimes muddy flavor of the flesh.

Tip: Rarely will you find catfish fillets with the skin on, unless you are cutting your own whole fish. This can be a drawback for grilling, as the flaky and delicate flesh can be difficult to remove from the grill in one piece. But if you use care and restrain yourself from fussing with it, grilled catfish can be a delightful addition to a Cobb or Caesar salad, or a filling for fish tacos.

Cobia

Also known as seriola or lemon fish, this popular sport fish is becoming widely available from responsible farming operations. Once limited to the Gulf states, where it is commonly caught, cobia is starting to be used everywhere by wise chefs who prize its firm, lean texture and culinary versatility. It has an assertive flavor, but is not fishy. Even in heavy spice, its sweet flavor shines through.

Tip: Cobia is great on the grill, and best cooked over a medium fire. It needs to be brined to retain its moisture but otherwise is very easy to cook; there's little danger of it falling to pieces. It is best paired with light fruitwood smoke, but this is one of few fish that can take a whiff of hickory or even mesquite to give it a spicy tang.

Fluke or summer flounder

There are many different varieties of flounder, all lumped together under the category of flatfish. Buying them is very confusing, as there are differing regional names for almost all the species, and the same name sometimes refers to two different fish—ask for more details at the fish counter. Unfortunately, many of the common flounder species are not all that common these days due to overfishing. But some are faring well and replenishing their numbers due to good management. Flatfish are not often considered for the grill, as the flake of the fillet is so small, but I like a challenge. When grilled whole, or inventively deboned, these make a great presentation.

Tip: The delicate flavor of flatfish is most often associated with the crisped golden crust of a fried fillet. When using the grill, the fish must be cooked with the skin on in order to avoid feeding your dinner to the embers. The bone structure of flatfish makes it very easy to remove the fillets from the skeleton once cooked. In fact, the fillets basically fall off the bone with little effort on the cook's part. See my recipe on page 167.

Halibut

Halibut is the largest member of the flatfish family and is caught on both coasts. There are different kinds of halibut, some sustainably caught, others in some distress. Look for Alaskan halibut as a best option. The season for halibut runs from spring through late autumn (grilling season!), and it is best when bought fresh, although previously frozen fillets can still yield delicious results.

Tip: Halibut can dry out very quickly, and though the snowy white flesh is beautifully flavored, it is not assertive by any means. Smoke can add a welcome dimension to the buttery flesh, but give it too much or cook it over too high a heat, and you may accentuate a not particularly tasty mineral tang in the flesh. So, cook it slowly, use a lightly flavored wood, and smoke with restraint.

Jacks

This is a big family of fish, including some that make for fantastic eating. My favorites for the grill are pompano and permit. The pompano is a smaller fish, usually about 1½ pounds, abundant on the East Coast, and best in the summer and autumn. Permit can grow quite a bit larger and is mostly a recreational catch, not usually found at market.

Tip: Pompano has a very clean flavor and grills well. It takes to smoke, especially maple and oak, and is great in hot-smoked preparations. Permit is also great on the grill. It cooks nearly the same as pompano, requiring just a little more time. For each of these, I prefer to grill without the skin. I find it tends to stick to the grate and, once cooked, does not peel off the flesh very well.

Mackarel

Mackerel is a delightfully tasty fish. It suffers from a widely held perception of being "fishy," a claim of which it is innocent. Smaller types are best and easiest to find at the market. While the brilliantly golden-spotted Spanish mackerel is my favorite, tiger-striped Boston mackerel is also good eats. The flesh of the Boston, though, is quite a bit softer and so needs to be treated with a light touch. King mackerel is a large fish mostly caught by recreational anglers, and to my taste, it should be avoided. The flavor can be overpowering, and it can be heavily laden with toxins.

Tip: When grilling mackerel, it is best to leave the skin on to keep the flesh from drying out. I like to peel it off before serving, but that is up to you. The fish can be grilled whole or as fillets. Mackerel is especially well suited to the deep smoke flavor imparted by a smoldering fire. When smoking mackerel, it must be hot-smoked so that the flesh is fully cooked. Mackerel is a fish that really sings when seasoned with freshly ground black pepper.

Mahimahi

This fish is quite popular on restaurant menus, as it pairs well with a host of flavors. It is a white-fleshed fillet with a full taste and big, moist flakes. It is caught in many waters in different seasons and so is easy to find fresh most of the year. It does not freeze well and can be tasteless if not pristinely fresh. Do not serve the skin of this fish; it is thick and inedible.

Tip: Mahimahi is great with a little smoke flavor, but nothing too strong. Frozen mahi tends to pick up a strong iodine flavor when smoked, another reason to look for fresh.

Sablefish

Also known as black cod, sablefish is one of the ocean's most wonderful delicacies. A bright white-fleshed fillet, usually no more than an inch thick, it has exceptional richness and flavor. This fish freezes well and so is a good choice year-round, but its prime season is between spring and late autumn.

Tip: Sablefish can be difficult to grill, due to its high fat content and small flake. Cooking one large portion with the skin on helps greatly to maintain the structure, but do remove the skin before serving. Sablefish is a good candidate for both cold- and hot-smoking. It is best when paired with hearty, but not overpowering, woods such as pecan, oak, or maple. When serving, grilled lemons or an acidic vinaigrette is a welcome balance to the rich fish.

Salmon

Wild salmon from the West Coast is one of our nation's piscatorial treasures. Sustainability can be an issue, so the origin of the product is important. See the Seafood Watch website for details (page 294).

Tip: Each of the different varieties of wild salmon has its own wonderful and unique characteristics. All take well to the grill, and all stand up to fairly strong smoke.

Chum

I think chum is most like the ubiquitous farmed Atlantic salmon, but only in texture and lightness of flavor. In quality, it soars above the farmed product. The taste, while light, is far more nuanced, and the fat is better integrated into the meat, which yields better cooking results.

Tip: Chum is not as fatty-rich as some of the other wild salmon varieties, so I prefer to cook these fillets slowly over moderate heat; it is best paired with a fruitwood smoke such as cherry or peach.

Coho

This is my favorite of all the salmon varieties. It has a wonderful balance of sweet flavor and robust, oily richness.

Tip: Coho cooks well over medium heat and is perfectly paired with peach wood smoke.

King

King is the richest and most expensive of the salmons. Worth every penny, it has a robust and haunting flavor that ranks in the top tier of culinary delights.

Tip: Full of fat, king salmon is best when cooked slowly to maintain moisture and impart smoke. But these fillets also sear well. So let them take on a little color over direct heat, then finish over low heat to create an inspiring crème-brûlée-like texture that is crisp and silken all at once.

Pink

The lightest of all the types, pink salmon is leaner and cleaner in flavor than its bigger brothers. These fish are usually used in canning, but when well cared for, the fresh product can be a joy to cook with.

Tip: Pink salmon takes well to hot-smoking. This salmon has the lowest fat content and, therefore, must be cooked with gentle heat in order to exalt its uniquely delicate characteristics.

Sockeye

This is the gamiest of the salmon species. It has a brilliant sunset-orange hue and a darker, more mineral flavor than the others.

Tip: This salmon, while high in fat, tastes lean, so it is imperative to cook it over low heat to retain as much moisture as possible.

Sardines

Sardines are the Ralph Nader of the seafood world. Everyone wants them around, but nobody really wants to fully endorse them. What we commonly refer to as sardines can in fact be many different species of fish. But the unifying qualities of size, shape, and oil content make this nearly a nonissue when it comes to cooking them.

Tip: I endorse sardines—always one of my favorite candidates for dinner! My preferred way to treat these little guys is to scale, gut, and salt-cure them. But they also do very well on the grill; see Atlantic Herring on page 153.

Snapper

Commonly snapper is referred to as red, but this is just one of the twenty or so species that are fished commercially. Many species are not very sustainable, while others are. Much of this depends on the area where they are caught, so please do a little research and support fishermen doing their part to protect and serve. Most snappers are pretty small at market, with fillets rarely bigger than a couple of pounds.

Tip: Given the relative thinness and fragile, flaky texture of snapper, it can be tough to grill. The skin is the key to holding it all together, literally. Always grill snapper skin side down and treat it lightly with smoke, if at all. Its supple yet delicate flavor can be overwhelmed easily.

Swordfish

Once faring not so well, this mighty icon of culinary fame has rebounded and is now considered to be sustainable enough to enjoy—once in a while. Check the Seafood Watch website (page 294) for up-to-date information. Cook swordfish with care and appreciation, making its appearance on your table a celebration. It is expensive, and it carries with it some concern about toxin buildup.

Tip: This fish takes to brine exceptionally well and needs a longer soak time than most, due to its dense flesh. It has an exceptional meaty texture and an unbelievable taste when fresh. When eaten near the shore, with salt breeze fueling a smoky driftwood fire, the moist and delicate nature of this powerful fish is a revelation. Cook it slowly, cook it flavorfully with continuous additions of hearty smoke from pecan or maple wood. And serve it with no more than a grilled lemon and a drizzle of fruity, delicate olive oil.

Tilapia

This is not the most flavorful of fishes, but it can make for an excellent meal. The fact that it does not have big flavor is a positive attribute for some folks, and it pairs well with nearly anything.

Tip: When grilling tilapia, it is important to keep it moist, so do not forget to brine it ahead of time. Cook it slowly, with little, if any, smoke. Too much, and the fish can pick up a metallic tang. Pairs best with a fatty sauce like aioli or vinaigrette.

Trout

Rainbow trout is farmed in many areas of this country and is a staple at fish markets. It's often sold butterflied, still whole but with all the bones removed.

Tip: Trout and smoke are good friends. The woodsy tones of the smoke accentuate the sweetness of its delicate meat. Apple and other fruitwoods make for the best pairings. Trout is almost always served with the skin on, which makes it easy to grill. The flesh cooks very quickly, so take care. My favorite preparations involve stuffing the cavity of a whole trout with citrus and herbs and then slowly grilling it over a smoky fire.

Tuna, red-fleshed varieties

There are a number of red-fleshed tunas, many of which are in dire straits as of now, bluefin chief among them. These monsters of the seas have been exploited mercilessly. But there are some good options available from a sustainability point of view that show relatively similar cooking traits, including bigeye and yellowfin. Check the Seafood Watch website (page 294) for up-to-date info.

Tip: Bigeye and yellowfin tuna respond well to a flavorful smoke such as cherry or peach wood. Both should be cooked very slowly to, at most, medium-rare doneness. When cooked beyond this point, tuna dries out quickly. Do not brine red tuna, as it changes the color and degrades the texture. Instead, give it a generous seasoning about 15 minutes before cooking.

Tuna, white-fleshed varieties

A disclaimer: white tuna, as a species, does not exist. I use the term here to refer to tunas that have a lighter character than the deeply red-colored tuna of sushi fame. This type has no less flavor and should be just as exalted. The best examples are albacore, skipjack, and wahoo. All exhibit the luxurious, fatty richness of their red-fleshed brethren, although they're not actually as fatty. The flesh is arranged in concentric rings that, when barely cooked, give the fish a silken texture. White tuna varieties are usually quite a bit cheaper than red tuna and are sometimes lower in possible toxin buildup.

Tip: "White tuna" is best when grilled to medium rare, as it begins to toughen and dry out quickly after that. It is also a good candidate for hot-smoking.

Calamari

It is best to find squid with the beautiful purplish skin still on—it's called "dirty squid" in the fish business. Not only can you better determine its freshness, but the thin membrane absorbs the flavors of the grill and makes for a stunning presentation too! Ask your fishmonger to order some for you, then have the squid cleaned of their insides, but be sure to tell them to leave the skin intact.

Tip: My favorite way to enjoy squid is to grill it whole, or almost whole—the head must be separated from the body to clean it, which leaves two pieces to grill. The tentacles char, so you get an amazing contrast in textures, from crisp darkened edges to the yielding, soft chew of the inner meat. The tubes are also beautiful as they puff up with the heat.

Clams

Clams are among the best options for sustainable seafood production. Farmed clams (mussels and oysters as well) are especially guilt-free eating, as they provide a host of environmental benefits. I like all types of clams, but the most common is the quahog. They come in a range of sizes, from small pasta size to the gigantic chowder clams. Smaller clams are better for the grill, as they have a more tender texture than larger ones that do better with longer cooking methods.

Tip: Grilled clams are a wonderful way to start a gathering. They tend to sit well on grill grates but might need to be propped against each other in order to maintain their precious juices once they open. Do not cook them over direct heat, as the shells can crack. You want medium heat for a few minutes, just until the shells open and they begin spitting juice. Pop them off the grill into a folded towel and use a shellfish knife to pry them open and cut the connecting muscles. Serve with melted butter or go nuts with flavors like paprika, tarragon, vinegars, or Mezcal Hot Sauce (page 277).

Crab, blue

This is the icon of the Chesapeake. I remember catching giant blue crabs as a child and the resulting all-night picking parties to freeze meat for the winter months. These crabs are found all along the East Coast and into the Gulf of Mexico, where they are an important fishery. Blue crab is available whole, soft-shelled (when molting), and as picked meat. Always look for domestic product, as it is far and away the best.

Tip: These crabs are not usually considered for the grill; only the soft-shell crabs can be fully cooked over it. Hard-shell crabs must be steamed to cook properly, but then can be reheated over the grill. Or try my recipe on page 187 for cooking crab cakes on the grill.

Crab, Dungeness

This is the favored crab of the Pacific Northwest and one that deserves its fame and culinary status. Usually they are available precooked and can be eaten chilled or gently warmed through.

Tip: I like to split the precooked crabs into quarters and give them a turn over a medium fire flavored with alder wood. I think they are best served with vinegar rather than a rich butter. Try them with Tarragon White Balsamic Condiment (page 278).

Crab, King

This is the prized catch of *The Deadliest Catch* fame and is almost exclusively sold precooked (and usually frozen). When warmed through, either by steaming or grilling, its flavor really blossoms.

Tip: I love the flavor king crab legs take on when the shells are charred over wood and then they're served with a rich aioli flavored with hot sauce or tarragon. After charring the shells, move the legs to the cooler part of the grill to ensure that they heat through without overcooking.

Lobster

Lobster is one of the most charismatic kinds of seafood and also one of the most expensive. But it is easy to cook, and a little bit can go a long way. I like to cook larger lobsters because you can feed many people with just one. For example, one 3-pound lobster can feed four people, but you would have to serve four 1¼-pounders to give the same crew their own lobsters.

Tip: Lobster is great on the grill, but it must first be blanched, then split open to expose the meat. Just a quick minute or two in boiling water, cut the lobster tip to tail, remove the sandy area just behind the eyes, and the lobster is ready for the grill. Brush it with oil and cook it cut side down to set the meat in the shell, then turn it and allow it to slowly roast on the cooler side of the grill until it's warmed through. I especially like to add pecan wood to the fire.

Mussels

Much like clams and oysters, mussels are an exceptional environmental choice. They are also one of the most consistent products available at market. They are farmed year-round in many areas, so there is a steady supply. And, due to the fact that they are harvested and shipped live, arriving at market within a day or two, they are usually quite fresh. Look for unbroken shells that are moist and tightly closed.

Tip: Mussels are not often considered for the grill, because they pop open when cooked and release all their tasty juices. If they're over a fire, this liquor is lost. But, despite the challenge, mussels are wonderful on the grill. They become drier, but they also pick up the light scent of the flames, and when paired with a fatty sauce such as aioli or a good vinaigrette, they can be amazing. A grill basket will help in the process, saving both time and the skin on your forearms.

Oysters

The oyster is the wine of the sea. Just as French chardonnay and pinot noir taste vastly different from California wines made with those same grapes, oysters reflect their provenance with startling disparity. Not only are there a few different species that are commonly available, they are farmed in thousands of waterways. Each area has its own distinct tidal patterns, nutrients, temperatures, etc. Each of these factors, just as in wine making, leads to different flavors in the shell.

Tip: I do believe that an oyster is at its best when served cold on the shell, shucked just moments before. But the cooked oyster does not lack for charm. The edges of the meat gently curl up, and the plump body takes on a demure beige hue as its liquor bubbles and turns white. You still want to be able to taste the oyster, whether it is poached, steamed, baked, or grilled, so treat added flavors with a light hand.

Scallops

The sweet flavor and modest yet pleasant chew make scallops the darling of many seafood lovers. But scallop populations have endured severe abuses at the hands of the fishing industry. The damage wrought by poor harvesting techniques and overfishing is not the fault of the fishermen alone; we, the consumers, ate their catch and so are equally responsible. Scallops can be hand-harvested by divers, who pluck each one from the seafloor. This method represents a small fraction of the scallops that make it to our tables, so beware of dubious "diver scallop" claims. However, some scallops are dredge-harvested in areas where the bottom terrain is sandy and highly resilient to dredging.

In short, it is a confusing issue. This is how I approach the matter. Support American fishermen, and support those who choose to take into account the health of the ecosystem. Also, regularly check the Seafood Watch website (see page 294) for the latest details. When buying scallops, look for ones that are brightly colored. They should be sweet smelling and tacky to the touch. They should appear moist, but there should be no exuded liquid.

Tip: Be sure to buy untreated scallops. Many scallops (and squid as well) are treated with a chemical brine that forces them to retain water. This damages the tissues, so when the scallop is exposed to heat, it immediately exudes moisture. This not only prevents you from getting any color on the scallop, but also the water (which you paid scallop price for) is lost. Untreated scallops are often labeled "dry-pack," but even that is no guarantee that they haven't taken a dunk.

Scallops are great for hot-smoking as well as for raw preparations. The smaller bay scallops when sold in the shell can be grilled; treat them like clams or oysters in any recipe.

Shrimp

America has a love affair with the shrimp. Unfortunately, the high demand for it has resulted in environmentally awful practices both for wild-caught and farmed shrimp. Wild shrimp, while now being harvested in increasingly responsible ways, suffer from a legacy of damaging impacts.

Imported farmed shrimp are usually not worth buying. Wild shrimp from American waters have some issues with bycatch, but are a product we should seek. Fresh shrimp, never frozen, truly are a delicacy worth enjoying in moderation. Also, look for the West coast delicacy Spot Prawns. Though only seasonally available, they have an intense, sweet flavor like that of lobster.

Tip: To grill, season the shrimp with salt and spices 20 minutes before cooking. Grill them just adjacent to the coals for only a few minutes. It is best to cook shrimp in their shells to give the meat more flavor and to retain moisture. Because this can make them messy to eat, save that treatment for informal gatherings where fingers are an acceptable utensil.

Shrimp are wonderful with fresh herbs such as tarragon, parsley, and chives and are very friendly with fresh garlic and citrus zest.

Arctic Char in the Style of Porchetta

In its true form, porchetta is a whole roast suckling pig seasoned generously with garlic, fennel, and rosemary. In this recipe, I borrow the term to reference its flavorings, as well as the contrast in textures it shares with traditional porchetta—moist, succulent flesh encased in crispy skin.

Arctic char has the perfect size fillet for this treatment, but you can substitute any wild salmon. I leave the rosemary out here, as its flavor can overpower seafood, but if you like that woodsy, musky element, try adding a touch of fresh thyme leaves. This makes for an elegant entrée to serve guests, as the visual presentation equals the aroma and flavor.

One 1¼-pound Arctic char fillet, pin bones discarded, skin removed and saved

1 tablespoon extra-virgin olive oil

2 cloves garlic, grated on a Microplane or very finely minced

1 teaspoon ground fennel seeds

½ cup fennel fronds (optional)

Freshly ground black pepper

Kosher salt

Lay the fillet on a cutting board and slice through the center horizontally to create two evenly thick sheets of fish. Arrange the pieces in a single layer in a shallow pan.

Heat the olive oil in a small sauté pan and add the garlic and fennel seeds. Cook over medium heat for just a few minutes, until the garlic no longer smells raw. Remove the pan from the heat. When the oil is cool, spoon it over the fillets, along with the fennel fronds, if using, a few cracks of pepper, and a generous seasoning of salt. Marinate the fish for at least 20 minutes and up to a couple of hours in the refrigerator.

Lay the fish skin, scale side down, on the cutting board and season it with a little salt. Arrange the fish pieces with the thick side of one on top of the thinner tail side of the other to form a layer that is relatively even in thickness throughout. Gently roll up the fillets and place them on the tail end of the skin. Holding the skin, begin to cover the fish with the skin, tightening the roll as you go. Some of the fish will stick out on the sides. Rub the fish skin with the oil remaining in the marinating dish.

Place the fish on the grill just adjacent to the coals of a medium fire (see page 15). Add some wood chips to the fire; I like hickory or mesquite, as either will complement the strong garlic flavor. Cover the grill, cook for about 10 minutes, then rotate the grill grate so that the other side of the fish is closest to the flame; do not move the fish itself. Cover and cook for another 10 minutes or so, adding more wood if necessary. When the fish is cooked, it will feel firm to the touch and the skin will be crisped and smoky brown.

Remove it from the grill and let it rest for 5 minutes before cutting it into 1-inch-thick slices. Serve immediately.

Serves 4

Grilled Bacon-and-Lemon-Wrapped Trout

Do you like trout? Do you like bacon? Do you like bacon when it gets an extra smoke on the grill? How about crisp bacon and moist, flaky, tender trout scented with caramelized lemon? *Yeah!* A slightly crunchy, tangy-sweet pomegranate-scallion relish adds a welcome bit of coolness.

2 rainbow trout, butterflied and boned (ask your fishmonger to do this)

Kosher salt

Freshly ground black pepper

8 strips smoked bacon

2 lemons, 1 sliced ⅛ inch thick, the other left whole

¼ cup pomegranate seeds

½ bunch scallions, trimmed and thinly sliced

1 teaspoon ground mace

2 tablespoons extra-virgin olive oil

Splay the trout and season the insides with salt and a scant bit of coarsely ground pepper, then close the fish. Lay out the strips of bacon in two rafts of 4 slices. Lay 3 lemon slices across the middle of each bacon raft. Lay the trout directly on top of the lemon slices. Fold the bacon around the trout to fully cover.

Grill the wrapped trout just adjacent to the coals of a medium fire (see page 15) flavored with the fruitwood of your choice and cover the grill. I prefer apple wood for this; trout and apple wood seem to have a special affinity. Cut the remaining lemon in half and place it on the grill directly over the fire, cut side down.

Check through the grill vent that the bacon is not causing any flare-ups. If it is, move the fish a little farther away from the fire. Cook until the bacon is crisp on the bottom, about 8 minutes, then flip the trout and cover the grill. Cook until the other side is crisp, another 5 to 6 minutes. Remove the lemon halves from the grill.

Meanwhile, mix the pomegranate seeds, scallions, mace, and olive oil together and stir to combine. Check the trout by gently prying open to see if the meat is evenly cooked throughout. If not, cover the grill for another 3 to 4 minutes.

Remove the fish from the grill using two spatulas to ensure that it does not fall apart. Garnish with the pomegranate relish and serve immediately with the lemon halves on the side.

Serves 4

Smoky Catfish and Trinity Black-Eyed Pea Salad

Catfish eat a diet of all sorts of stuff and can exhibit flavors that bear evidence of that. A common complaint of diners is that the fish tastes muddy or slightly musky. Good producers have found ways to minimize this while still maintaining the ecological integrity of their operations. But unfortunately, much of this information is not passed on to consumers, so I will share a few tips for making the most of what is available.

Catfish benefits from a brief swim in a salty brine before cooking. This improves not only the flavor but also the moisture content of the finished product. With catfish, the addition of a little acid to the brine can help to draw out undesirable flavors. This is commonly seen in Southern cooking, in which the fish is given a salted buttermilk bath before being breaded and fried.

All cultures have their building blocks of flavor; in French cooking, it's the mirepoix, a sauté of chopped onion, celery, and carrot. The foundation of many Latino dishes is sofrito, whose composition changes with each country. For the Creole and Cajun cooking of Louisiana, the "holy trinity" of celery, bell pepper, and onion is the starting point of most savory dishes. This salad is in homage to that trinity.

One 15-ounce can black-eyed peas, drained and rinsed under cold running water

1 red bell pepper, seeded and cut into thin strips

1 small red onion, sliced super thin

3 stalks celery, thinly sliced

1 tablespoon white balsamic vinegar or good-quality white wine vinegar

2 tablespoons extra-virgin olive oil

Kosher salt

Leaves from 4 sprigs fresh mint, torn

1 pound U.S. catfish fillets, soaked in Fish Brine (page 263) with a squeeze of ½ orange or lemon added

To make the salad, mix the black-eyed peas with the pepper strips, onion, celery, vinegar, and olive oil in a medium bowl. Season to taste with salt and sprinkle with the mint. Toss to combine and let sit at least 15 minutes for the flavors to combine.

Place the catfish on the grill away from a medium fire (see page 15) and add a handful of wood chunks, preferably a robustly scented wood such as hickory or mesquite. Cover the grill and cook for 12 to 15 minutes, depending on the thickness of the fish and intensity of the fire. The fish is done when it flakes under gentle pressure and has an amber, smoky hue.

Serve the catfish hot off the grill on a bed of the salad. Any leftover fish can be flaked into the salad, refrigerated, and served the next day.

Serves 4

INGREDIENTS I LOVE:
WHITE BALSAMIC VINEGAR

This vinegar has an incredible balance of sweet and tart. It is made from the same grapes as traditional dark balsamic, but the juice is boiled only for a slight reduction and to block any fermentation. The resulting juice is then aged for one year to yield a very mellow but vibrant acidity and fresh fruit aromas. This vinegar makes a perfect sauce on its own; I particularly like it infused with herbs, as in my Tarragon White Balsamic Vinegar Condiment on page 278.

filleting the fish

seasoning the fish

Grilled Whole Summer Flounder with Smoked Tomato Sauce

Flounder is a favorite of seafood lovers everywhere. However, many species have been overfished, and most are not considered sustainable. The summer flounder (which is a type of flounder, not a seasonal reference) is doing quite well, and the fishery is rebounding. Also called fluke, it is one of the tastier varieties. To be sure that you are getting a summer flounder, you can use this trick: hold the fish with the belly down and the mouth facing away from you. If the colored skin side of the fish is on the left side, then it is a summer flounder. But if the nonpigmented side is on the left, then it is another variety, and you might want to avoid it.

Because of its thin fillets and small flake, this fish is not typically grilled. But when grilled whole and then delicately filleted at the table, it makes for a wonderful presentation. Ask your fishmonger to take off the head and remove the stomach. If you feel like giving your fishmonger a challenge, you can also ask for the fish to be "glove boned." This is when the bones are removed through the front end, leaving the fish otherwise intact. It makes seasoning and serving much easier.

One 2- to 3-pound summer flounder, head and stomach removed

Kosher salt

2 tablespoons extra-virgin olive oil, or oil from Smoke-Dried Tomatoes (page 281)

Juice of 1 lemon

6 Smoke-Dried Tomato halves

Lay the whole fish, colored side up, on the grill away from the coals of a medium fire (see page 15). If you're cooking a glove-boned fish, first season the fillets with salt. Add a handful of wood chunks to the fire (I particularly like alder wood with this) and cover the grill. Adjust the air intake to just a sliver and cook for 25 to 30 minutes, depending on the size of the fish and intensity of the fire. When cooked through, the skin will easily peel away, and the flesh will be white and will flake under gentle pressure.

Meanwhile, make the sauce. Heat the oil in a small saucepan over medium heat, then add the lemon juice and tomatoes. Cook just until the tomatoes begin to break down, about 3 minutes. Remove the sauce from the heat and season with a pinch of salt. Mash the mixture with a fork to integrate the ingredients.

Transfer the fish to a platter by either transferring the whole fish or filleting it on the grill and transferring just the meat. If you're cooking a glove-boned fish, transfer the whole fish, peel back the skin, then serve. For a bone-in fish, peel back the skin, remove the fillets, and, using a thin spatula, gently separate one fillet at a time running down the length of the fish. Lift the fillet to the platter. Repeat with the second fillet. Now you can easily peel back the exposed spine, using the spatula to separate it from the bottom fillets. Lift the remaining meat from the skin. Remove all skin and bones from the grill while it is still warm and discard them. You do not want to wait to do this later, trust me.

Season the fish with a little salt, then spoon the sauce on top and serve.

Serves 4

Grilled Pacific Halibut with Pistachio Butter

Halibut does well on the grill, especially when infused with a fruity smoke. It is a delicate and flaky white-fleshed flatfish and must be handled with great care so as not to lose pieces of it to the fire. Also, it is essential that you get a fillet that still has the skin on to help keep things intact and to retain moisture. When cooking a delicate fish, I like to work with one large piece; it holds together better, and you are handling it only once, as opposed to having to deal with each portion separately. It looks great on a platter too—one big, thick fillet gently colored by the wood smoke, with the bright pistachio butter melting over the top.

Look for Alaskan halibut, as it is a sustainably managed fishery. But check regularly with the Seafood Watch website (see page 294) for the most up-to-date information. Atlantic halibut is not doing so well right now, but let's hope that, within the lifespan of this book, that will change.

One 1¼-pound skin-on Alaskan halibut fillet, soaked for 30 minutes in Fish Brine (page 263)

½ tablespoon extra-virgin olive oil

½ cup Pistachio Compound Butter (page 275), at room temperature

Remove the fish from the brine and pat it dry. Rub the olive oil over the fillet.

Place the fish skin side down on the grill, as far as possible from the coals of a small fire (see page 15). Add fruitwood chips to the coals; I prefer cherry or peach. Cover the grill and cook for about 20 minutes, depending on the heat of the fire. Do not rotate the fish and do not flip it. To test for doneness, gently insert a small knife into the center of the fillet and take a peek. If it is evenly colored throughout and the tip of the knife is hot when you pull it out, the fish is done.

Remove the entire fillet from the grill to a platter using two spatulas to evenly support it. The skin should not stick at all, but if it does, use the spatulas to separate the fillet from the skin and remove only the meat. You can go back for the skin later, as you won't be serving it anyway. If the skin does come off the grill easily, hold the fish over the platter at a slight angle and peel the skin away; it will come right off.

Immediately top the fish with the pistachio butter and serve.

Serves 4

Whole Roasted Striped Bass

On the East Coast, striped bass is king. It is one of the great success stories of sustainable fisheries management, as multiple states joined together to protect this delicious and commercially valuable species. The striped bass, known regionally by many names, such as rockfish, greenback, and striper, is one of the best eating fish on any coast. The flesh is a soft, tender, and flaky wonder. The thick skin crisps well, but the large flake of the flesh is what really inspires chefs, anglers, and home cooks alike.

One 4-pound striped bass, gutted and scaled

1 recipe Herb Marinade (page 269)

1 recipe Preserved Lemon Gremolata (page 284) or Red Wine Sauce (page 274)

Cut three shallow incisions into each side of the fish. Place it in a large shallow baking dish and pour the marinade over it. Turn the fish a couple of times to coat, then let it marinate in the refrigerator for at least 4 hours and up to 1 day, turning it several times.

Prepare a large fire (see page 15) and let it burn down to embers. Add five or six fist-size chunks of a lightly flavored wood such as pecan, apple, or cherry. Once the wood has caught fire, choke the airflow to a sliver and place the fish on the coolest part of the grill. Cover the grill and let it cook for 25 minutes. Check the fire and add more wood if necessary. Cook for another 20 minutes with the grill covered.

Remove the whole fish from the grill using two spatulas to make sure that it doesn't fall apart. Place the fish on a platter and let it rest for at least 10 minutes. Remove the top fillet by gently running a spatula down the spine to separate the flesh from the bone. Gently lift the fish off the bone and transfer it to a platter; remove any rib bones. Spread half the chosen sauce over the fillet. Lift the head of the fish away from the bottom fillet, using the spatula to help pry the bones free. Once these are removed, transfer the second fillet to the platter and spoon the remaining sauce on top. Serve immediately.

Serves 4

Grilled Spanish Mackerel with Orange-Tarragon Salsa

When cooking mackerel on the grill, it is best to leave the skin on to prevent the flesh from drying out. I like to peel it off before serving, but that is up to you.

2 oranges

½ red onion or 2 shallots, finely diced

Leaves from 6 sprigs fresh tarragon, chopped

1 tablespoon extra-virgin olive oil

Pinch of kosher salt

One 1¼-pound skin-on mackerel fillet, soaked in Fish Brine (page 263)

Freshly ground black pepper

To make the salsa, peel the oranges and cut them into segments; cut each segment into thirds and combine these with the onion, tarragon, and olive oil in a small bowl. Season with the salt and toss well.

Remove the fillet from the brine and pat it dry. Season the fish with coarsely ground pepper. Mackerel has enough fat that it will not need to be oiled before grilling if your grates are well seasoned. Place the fillet, skin side down, on the grill away from the coals of a small fire (see page 15) and add a few fruitwood chips to the fire. Cover the grill and cook for about 10 minutes, depending on the thickness of the fish and the heat of the fire. The fish is cooked when it is no longer opaque, has turned an even beige color, and the flesh flakes under gentle pressure. Transfer it to a platter.

Spoon the salsa over the fish and serve immediately.

Serves 4

Cold-Smoked Alaskan King Salmon Three Ways

Cold-smoked salmon is what most people think of as lox. When I was a graduate assistant at the Culinary Institute of America, I had to smoke salmon, ten to thirty sides of it a day. It is a process that takes a couple of days, and so I was always mindful of how much I had and what stage of the process it had reached. In the cold, cold fish-cutting kitchen, one of the few pleasures was the ever-present wispy smoke from the smoker that was in nearly constant use. That warm aroma reminded me that somewhere, someone was warm, with toasty toes baking by a fire.

King salmon is best for cold-smoking because of its super-high fat content, which makes the final product moist and decadently rich, but coho also works well, as does a very high-quality, responsibly farmed Atlantic salmon. Only the most pristine, absolutely fresh fish will do for this preparation. It is not worth the time and effort if the fish is not perfectly fresh.

A whole side of smoked salmon is an investment, and although it keeps well in the fridge, it can be tough to use all of it. So here I include a couple of flavorings that make an attractive and interesting trio for a party platter—or just for you so that you don't tire of the same seasonings. They are variations of recipes I made while at the Culinary Institute, so credit for these ideas goes to the wonderful chef instructors of that school.

1 side skin-on Alaskan king salmon (about 6 pounds), scaled, pin bones left in

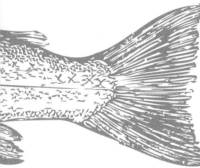

CLASSIC CURE:

3½ cups kosher salt

1 cup sugar

1½ tablespoons ground mace

1½ tablespoons ground coriander

1½ tablespoons onion powder

Pinch of cayenne pepper

1 tablespoon Pernod, sambuca, bourbon, or vermouth (depends on your preference)

BEET-HORSERADISH FLAVORING:

1 large beet, trimmed and scrubbed thoroughly

2 tablespoons water

2 tablespoons prepared horseradish

Fronds from 2 sprigs fresh dill, finely chopped

PASTRAMI FLAVORING:

3 tablespoons molasses

1 teaspoon smoked sweet paprika

2 teaspoons crushed coriander seeds

1 tablespoon coarsely ground black pepper

For the Classic Cure, stir together the salt, sugar, mace, coriander, onion powder, and cayenne. On a tray big enough to hold the salmon, sprinkle a light dusting of the cure, about ½ cup, where the salmon will be placed. Using a very sharp knife, make three or four long, shallow incisions in the skin of the salmon to allow the cure to penetrate evenly. Place the salmon, skin side down, on top of the cure mix. Cover the salmon with the remaining cure mix, making a layer about ½ inch thick. It can be a little lighter toward the tail, where the flesh is thinner.

Place the salmon in the refrigerator, uncovered, and let it cure for about 18 hours.

After the curing time is over, gently wash the fillet under cold running water. This is best done on the tray so that you are not holding the fish, thereby risking a tear in the flesh. Once all the cure mix has been washed away, pat the fish dry and place it on a wire rack. Brush it with the chosen alcohol, which will aid in the evaporation of any surface moisture. Place the fish back into the refrigerator in an area with high airflow. Let it dry for at least a day. This process creates what is called a pellicle—proteins drawn out by the cure mix dry on the surface and form a tacky film which the smoke will adhere to.

In a smoker (a traditional grill is usually too small for this operation, unless you have a mack daddy grill), light a small fire (see page 15). When it has burned to coals, place the fish as far away from the heat as possible. Place a flameproof bowl filled with ice directly over the fire to cool the rising smoke. Add a handful of wood chips or sawdust to the coals and cover the grill or shut the smoker to capture the flavorful gray, billowing smoke. I like to use chips or dust for this, since these add little heat as they smolder. And the purpose here is to add the maximum smoke flavor without ever heating the fish past room temperature so that all the luscious fat stays within the flesh and the final product is silken and moist. I prefer to use fruitwoods for smoking salmon, especially peach, cherry, and apricot—sometimes I throw in a bit of apple, though a full apple smoke can be too much. On the West Coast, alder wood is the preferred flavor, which I like very much. I have also found that old wine barrel staves add an amazing flavor. These barrels are almost always made of oak, typically a rather assertive flavored smoke, but having been softened by the aging of wine, they offer a mature and complex tone that is beguiling.

Continuously monitor the fire to ensure that it getting the fuel it needs but isn't getting too hot. The salmon is flavored after 30 minutes of constant smoke, but I think that it really begins to reach its peak after 1¼ hours but before 2 hours. After that, the fish is at a temperature that makes it more likely to begin to cook.

Remove the fish from the smoker and, using a pair of tweezers, pull out the pin bones, which will now be exposed and quite easy to remove. If you're using just the classic recipe with no additional flavorings, wrap the fish tightly in plastic and refrigerate it overnight.

The salmon is now ready to serve, or you can flavor it. If you're going to flavor it, cut the salmon fillet into three equal portions. Wrap one portion tightly in plastic and refrigerate it until you're ready to serve.

For the Beet-Horseradish Flavoring, grate the beet over the smallest holes of a box grater into a bowl. Mix the shredded beet with the water, horseradish, and dill. Place one portion of the salmon on top of a sheet of plastic wrap. Coat the flesh side of the salmon with the beet mixture and fold the plastic

wrap tightly around the fish to gently press the flavorings into the fish. Wrap tightly again with plastic and put on a plate in the refrigerator. The flavor and color will take after one day, but the salmon is best after 2 to 3 days. After this period, unwrap and gently wash off the fish.

For the Pastrami Flavoring, mix all the ingredients in a small bowl and add a couple of drops of water if necessary to thin the mixture to a spreadable paste. Place one portion of the salmon on top of a sheet of plastic wrap. Slather the flesh side of the salmon with the flavoring and tightly fold the plastic around the fish. Wrap it tightly again with plastic and put it on a plate in the refrigerator. The flavors will take after a day, but the salmon is best after 2 to 3 days. After this period, unwrap and either gently wash off the fish or leave the flavoring on the fish for visual and textural contrast.

To slice smoked salmon, use a long, thin, flexible knife. Start at the tail end of the fillet and, with a single, smooth stroke, slice the salmon paper-thin at about a 30-degree angle. This takes practice to master, but the good news is that the salmon will be delicious no matter how it is sliced, and your friends will all be super impressed.

Salmon cured, smoked, and, if desired, flavored, will keep for up to to 2 weeks in the refrigerator and up to 4 months in the freezer.

Makes about 6 pounds
(but the recipe can easily be adjusted for smaller quantities)

Classic Cure

Beet-Horseradish (Flavoring)

174

Maple
Cure

Orange-Scented Bluefish

Bluefish is remarkably delicious and versatile. It is wonderful on the grill, its fatty richness complemented by the flavor of wood smoke. That richness ("oiliness" to the minds of some) causes many people to shun bluefish and other similar ocean brethren. All I can say is, oh well, more for me. Here orange zest provides an acidic tang that helps to balance the flavors, and the slow, low heat of the smoldering wood cooks the fish without drying it out.

One 1¼-pound skin-on bluefish fillet, soaked in Fish Brine (page 263)

1 tablespoon extra-virgin olive oil

Finely shredded zest of 1 orange

Remove the fish from the brine and pat it dry. Brush it with a mixture of the olive oil and orange zest. Place the fish, skin side down, on the grill away from the coals of a small fire (see page 15). Add a few chunks of wood to the coals and cover the grill. For bluefish, I prefer a fruit or nut wood such as peach, pecan, apple, or cherry. Orange wood is also a fun choice. Close the air intake to just a sliver and cook for 12 to 15 minutes, depending on the thickness of the fillet and intensity of the fire. When the fish is cooked, it will have a beautiful rusty hue and the meat will flake under gentle pressure. Gently remove the fillets to a platter and serve immediately. I like to remove the skin of bluefish and the underlying darkly colored bloodline just beneath it, as these can have strong flavors that some guests do not appreciate. It also helps to remove some of the toxins that are a concern with bluefish, as they tend to aggregate just under the skin.

Serves 4

Grilled Tuna Melt

Tuna is a tricky subject. We regularly hear stories of environmental abuses perpetrated by some in the tuna industry. Some of the tuna that is canned is not taken from the sea in the best of ways. But an increasing number of companies are beginning to make serious and meaningful advances to improve their practices, and these companies should be supported. There are also a number of brands that are highly sustainable and make their products in the best way possible. These products tend to cost a bit more, and they should. Those extra dollars are supporting small-scale fishing communities committed to creating an exemplary model for others to follow. Visit the Seafood Watch website (see page 294) to learn more about this topic, as they have the most up-to-date information on what to look for when buying tuna.

This dish is a fun take on the classic. The tuna can be replaced with canned mackerel or pink salmon for an equally delicious and healthful result.

Two 5-ounce cans skipjack or albacore tuna (look for a can that says pole- or troll-caught)

2 tablespoons mayonnaise

1 teaspoon ground mace

1 teaspoon ground coriander

Kosher salt

4 slices pumpernickel bread

6 ounces cheddar cheese (I prefer a sharp white cheddar)

Open and drain the tuna. Combine it in a medium bowl with the mayonnaise, spices, and a pinch of salt. Mix thoroughly to combine, then spread it evenly on all the bread slices. Cut the cheese into ¼-inch-thick slices and layer them over the tuna.

Set the open-faced sandwiches on the grill away from the coals of a medium fire (see page 15). Add a few wood chips to the fire and cover the grill. (I really like apple wood for this.) Cook for 10 minutes or so, then check on the sandwiches. The bread should be lightly toasted on the bottom, and the cheese completely melted. In the least obvious way possible, stick your finger into one of the sandwiches (maybe the one you serve yourself!) to make sure that the tuna has heated all the way through. If the sandwiches need more time, cover the grill and give it another 5 minutes. Carefully remove the sandwiches from the grill and serve them immediately.

Serves 4

Grilled Tuna Spines

I first met Chris Cosentino in Turin, Italy, where we were both attending the biannual Terra Madre conference. By luck of the draw, I was selected to share a room with Chris, Rocky Maselli (a culinary phenom working in Oregon), and Mourad Lahlou, the soulful and masterful hand behind Aziza in San Francisco. We were all strangers to each other, but by week's end, we had become lifelong friends.

On a trip to San Francisco, I made my way to Chris's iconic restaurant Incanto in Noe Valley, where he served me a dish of tuna spines, presented like ribs, with a fragrant, crunchy topping of mint, capers, garlic, and chile. Chris told me that tuna spines are considered a delicacy in Sicily. But in all my research, I have never seen mention of this. No recipes, no references, no acknowledged culinary history. So I borrow this recipe from Chris. And to him, my friend, goes all credit.

The introduction of a small amount of wood smoke with muscular taste like mesquite or hickory is a welcome gilding of the lily.

6 pounds tuna spines, cut into 3-rib sections (any good fishmonger can get the spines for you with a couple of days' advance notice)

Kosher salt

1 cup extra-virgin olive oil

2 tablespoons capers, drained

Leaves from 1 bunch fresh mint

3 cloves garlic, sliced super thin

8 dried piri piri or Calabrian chiles or 1 tablespoon crushed red pepper

Season the spines generously with salt and drizzle them with 2 tablespoons of the olive oil. Let them sit in the refrigerator for at least 20 minutes and up to 4 hours.

In a small sauté pan, heat the remaining olive oil over high heat, Add the capers and cook until they begin to crisp, 5 to 7 minutes. Add the mint, garlic, and chiles. Cook until the mint leaves are crisp and the garlic slices are golden brown, about 5 minutes. Remove the pan from the heat and set it aside.

Sear the spines directly over the coals of a large fire (see page 15) for 5 to 7 minutes. Rotate the grill grate so that the spines are away from the coals and continue to cook for another 10 to 15 minutes.

When the spines begin to char and the meat along the ribs is cooked to a dark gray, cut each vertebra along the transparent line that separates each joint. Lay the sections flat on a platter with the jelly-like marrow exposed. Spoon the hot oil over the joints, evenly distributing the mint, garlic, and capers. Season with a generous sprinkling of salt and serve immediately. (The rib meat attached to the bones is delicious, and the marrow is best eaten with a few bits of the garnish. This is a messy undertaking, just like pork ribs. So don't invite the Queen of England, or anyone you know to be particularly in favor of decorum over deliciousness.

Serves 4 (an adventurous 4, that is)

Grilled Sardines with Lime-Almond Dressing

Fresh sardines are a true delicacy if you can find them. Most stores with a fresh fish counter don't carry them regularly, but if you ask a couple of days ahead of time, they should be able to get them for you.

These delicious, roughly 6-inch-long fish are not at all comparable to the unfortunately much-maligned canned version. They are briny and sweet, packed with ocean flavor. Your fishmonger should be able to do most of the work of scaling and gutting the fish for you, but the task is easily accomplished by scraping with your thumbnail from the tail to the head under cold running water. The belly cavity is simple to remove with a paring knife.

Like many full-flavored fish, sardines are well suited to a few cracks of fresh pepper. The dressing has some acidic punch to help tame the richness of the fish.

1¼ pounds fresh sardines, scaled and gutted

Kosher salt

Freshly ground black pepper

1 large egg yolk

Juice of 1 lime

¼ cup Chunky Almond Oil (page 272)

2 teaspoons extra-virgin olive oil

Season the fish generously with salt and a few cracks of pepper. Let sit for at least 20 minutes at room temperature while the salt works its magic.

In a small bowl, whisk together the egg yolk, lime juice, and a pinch of salt. Slowly whisk in the almond oil in a steady stream. When all the almond oil is added, the sauce should be slightly creamy in texture. Set aside.

Brush the fish with the olive oil and place it directly over the coals of a medium fire (see page 15) flavored with a few chunks of oak. Let the fish sit undisturbed for 3 minutes as the skin chars and begins to crackle. Rotate the grill grate so the fish are away from the heat; cover the grill. Cook until the flesh flakes with gentle pressure, about another 7 minutes, depending upon the heat of the grill.

Transfer the fish to a platter, placing them charred sides up. Spoon the dressing over the hot fish and serve immediately.

Serves 4

Grilled Fish Tacos

Fish tacos have recently gained great popularity in this country, which unfortunately means there are a lot of bad fish tacos out there—fish seasoned beyond recognition with powerful flavors like chili powder and cumin. A good fish taco is a perfectly textured corn tortilla filled with fresh ingredients that work in harmony. I add a nontraditional touch in the form of fennel, which, while unexpected, is a welcome textural addition.

1 small serrano or jalapeño pepper, seeded and finely minced

1 small red onion, finely diced

1 tablespoon fresh orange juice

Juice and finely shredded zest of 1 lime

Kosher salt

1 pint Sun Gold or other cherry tomatoes, cut in half

Leaves from ½ bunch fresh cilantro, finely chopped

3 teaspoons extra-virgin olive oil

One 1¼-pound fish fillet (my favorites for this are Spanish mackerel, pole-caught mahimahi or albacore tuna, coho salmon, or catfish), soaked in Fish Brine (page 263)

16 fresh soft corn tortillas

1 head frisée lettuce, separated into leaves

1 small bulb fennel, stalks discarded, shaved paper-thin (this is best done on a mandoline)

Combine the chile pepper, onion, orange juice, lime juice, and a good pinch of salt in a medium bowl. Toss to combine and let sit for 5 to 10 minutes. This step will help to coax more flavor from the chile and better integrate its flavor throughout the salsa, which also helps to soften its heat. Add the tomatoes, cilantro, and 2 teaspoons of the olive oil and toss to combine. Season with another small pinch of salt (but keep the salsa a little underseasoned so the tomatoes retain more of their juice).

Remove the fish from the brine and pat it dry. Mix the lime zest with the remaining 1 teaspoon olive oil and brush it over the fillet. Cook on the coolest part of the grill over a medium fire (see page 15). I like to use mesquite for this, but sparingly, just a few chips thrown in a couple of minutes before adding the fish. Cover the grill and cook for 10 to 15 minutes, depending on the type of fish you are using and the intensity of the fire. The fish is done when it flakes easily under gentle pressure. Remove it to a platter and let it rest. If the fish was cooked with its skin, gently peel off and discard the skin.

Cook the corn tortillas a few at a time directly over the fire to lightly char them on both sides. Once all the tortillas have been grilled, wrap them in a napkin to keep them moist and warm.

With a fork, gently flake the fish into small pieces and put it in a bowl to preserve the heat and juices. Serve everything family style and let everyone make their own tacos. I like to use two stacked tortillas with a few frisée leaves on the bottom, then the fish, the fennel, and finally a dollop of salsa.

Serves 4

Smoky Fish Stew

Few things are more appealing than a giant steaming pot of impeccably fresh seafood stewed together. And this dish will deliver a big wow factor when you unveil it from the grill. Most of the work is done ahead of time in the kitchen; all you need is a fire at the right temperature to throw the pot onto, and in twenty minutes, you've got a feast.

2 cups dry white wine, such as chardonnay or sauvignon blanc

One 1½-pound lobster

2 teaspoons fennel seeds

2 cloves

1 dime-size knob fresh ginger, thinly sliced

One 8-ounce bottle clam juice

Kosher salt

Pinch of saffron (about 10 threads; optional)

2 pounds mussels, scrubbed and debearded (discard any that won't close)

50 littleneck clams, scrubbed thoroughly (discard any with broken shells or that won't close)

1 pound fish fillets, such as striped bass, bluefish, or amberjack, cut into 1-inch pieces

½ cup Lemony Aioli (page 71)

1 baguette

In a large flameproof stew pot, bring the wine to a boil. Add the lobster, cover, and bring back to a boil. Cook 1 minute more; then remove the lobster, reserving the wine in the pot. Cool the lobster until it is comfortable to handle.

Meanwhile, add the fennel seeds, cloves, ginger, clam juice, a pinch of salt, and, if using, the saffron to the wine; bring it to a low simmer.

Holding the lobster over a tray to collect the juice, separate the tail from the head by gripping both ends firmly to rotate and pull them apart. Hold the tail in both hands with the shell up and head end closest to you. Gripping with your fingers under the shell, push down with both hands to crack the shell. Reserve the meat and the shells separately. Crack the claws and knuckles using the back of a knife; remove the meat. Tear off the legs and put them with the other shell pieces. Scrape out the inside of the head of the lobster, saving the thin sheets of meat lying just under the shell but discarding the other contents. Also discard the tomalley and coral roe if it is present. Chop all the meat into bite-size pieces and place them in a covered dish in the fridge. Add the shells and any collected juice to the wine in the pot and simmer for 20 minutes; strain the broth and discard the solids. Remove the pot from the stove and add the mussels, clams, and fish pieces. Toss to evenly distribute.

Place the whole pot on the grill directly over the coals of a medium fire (see page 15); add alder, apple, or cherry wood chunks to the coals. Cover the grill and let cook for 10 to 15 minutes, then carefully stir the contents of the pot. Add the reserved lobster chunks and cover the grill. Cook until the clams are almost all open, about another 10 minutes.

Ladle out portions into bowls (discarding any mussels or clams that haven't opened). Top each serving with a big dollop of the aioli. Serve with torn pieces of baguette to sop up the broth and a big bowl to collect all the empty shells.

Serves 4 to 6

Grilled Oysters with Smoked Lemon Aioli

Oysters are, to my mind, at their best when raw, pristine little gifts delivered on the half shell. But then my friend Charlie Williams sent along a BBQ Oyster Grill for me to try out. One of my only complaints about grilling oysters is that they tend to lose too much of their precious liquor because they don't sit easily on the grill grates. Well, Mr. Charlie has solved this little problem (see Sources, page 296). It is hard to make this aioli in small quantities, so I just upped the number of oysters. You don't mind, do you?

1 lemon
1 large egg yolk
Kosher salt
1 teaspoon maple syrup
Pinch of ground mace
1 clove garlic, peeled
2 cups canola oil
36 deep-cupped oysters, scrubbed well

For the aioli, place the whole lemon in the coals of a medium fire (see page 15) flavored with fruitwood and roast until it is soft and oozing its juice, about 20 minutes. Or grill 2 lemon halves directly over the coals until deeply caramelized, turning to cook the skin side for a few minutes as well. Let the lemon cool to room temperature.

Squeeze the grilled lemon juice into a blender and add the more roasted half of the lemon peel (yes, the entire lemon half, peel and all). Add the egg yolk, a pinch of salt, the maple syrup, mace, and garlic. Blend on low speed to make a thick paste. Still on low speed, begin to add the canola oil in a slow, steady stream. Do not rush this process. Continue to add the oil in steady stream as the sauce begins to thicken. If it becomes too thick, add a few drops of water and continue with the oil until all of it has been incorporated. The texture should be smooth but thick, just slightly thinner than jarred mayonnaise. Cover tightly and refrigerate until needed or up to 2 days (any longer than that, and the garlic flavor gets too strong).

Have an oyster knife and thick towel at hand. Place 9 whole oysters with the deep cup side down on the BBQ Oyster Grill or on the grill grate directly over the coals of a large fire (see page 15). As the oysters cook, they will begin to spit their liquor; this means they're ready. As this happens, remove the cooked oyster and replace it with a new one.

Hold the cooked oyster with the towel and insert the knife in the small opening between the shells. Run the knife along the top shell to release it and then discard. Use the knife to cut under the oyster in a scooping motion to sever the bottom muscle. Top each oyster with a dollop of cold aioli, and eat hot (and cold) right away. Continue until all the oysters are eaten, but expect your guests to be a little disappointed when they are gone!

Serves as many as you want (recipe is for 3 dozen oysters and aioli to match)

Pine Bough–Roasted Mussels

This is a dish that captured my heart many years ago. I read about it, *éclade des moules*, in some novel, possibly Dickens or Eleanor Clark. This preparation has roots in a French seaside tradition of a large cookout similar to a New England clambake.

Pine is usually avoided in barbecue circles, as the resinous smoke can be overpowering and bitter. But given the quick cooking time of mussels, this highly aromatic and dense smoke is a perfect touch. I like to serve these with tarragon aioli, as the cool flavor of tarragon softens the pitch flavor of pine. But any way you present this, it is an impressive undertaking and one that is sure to have all your guests gathered around the grill to watch.

The Normandy region on the northern coast of France is famous for its fermented apple cider. Effervescent, dry, and low in alcohol, it is an amazingly great partner to this dish.

1 large egg yolk

1 tablespoon white wine vinegar

1 clove garlic, grated on a Microplane or very finely minced

Leaves from 8 sprigs fresh tarragon, chopped

Kosher salt

2 cups canola oil

4 to 6 pine boughs, enough to cover the grill surface

4 pounds mussels, thoroughly scrubbed and debearded (discard any that won't close)

Mix the egg yolk, vinegar, garlic, tarragon, and a pinch of salt in a medium bowl. Whisk to combine, then begin to add the canola oil in a slow, steady stream. Continue whisking as you add the oil and, remember, patience is the key. The sauce will thicken as you add the oil until it is a smooth mayonnaise; if it gets too thick, add a couple of drops of water to thin it out. Cover tightly and refrigerate until ready to serve or up to 2 days (any longer than that, and the garlic flavor gets too strong).

Place the pine boughs over a medium fire (see page 15) in which the coals have been spread out around the base grate. As soon as the pine begins to sizzle and release wisps of steam and smoke, scatter the mussels over the boughs and cover the grill. The pine will smolder and smoke, perfuming the mussels as they pop open. Uncover the grill and check them after 7 minutes. Remove the mussels that have opened, which should be most of them. Continue to cook those that haven't opened for another 5 minutes or so. Discard any that insist on remaining closed.

Place one of the charred pine boughs on a platter and pile the mussels around it. Provide toothpicks and serve them with a bowl of the aioli.

Serves 4 (but quantities can easily be increased)

Citrus-Marinated Diver Scallops

I do not often eat scallops, as the portion sizes are too big in many restaurants. First, I don't think that we need to eat very much protein, but second, scallops are so rich that I usually don't want more than one or two. In this dish, the orange zest helps to balance that richness while also accentuating the sweetness of the meat. And when cooked over a smoky fire, the resulting morsels are a beautiful golden hue with specks of fiery orange.

1 pound U-10 scallops
(U-10 is a size measure and means under 10 per pound)

Finely shredded zest of 1 orange

1 tablespoon extra-virgin olive oil

Kosher salt

Combine the scallops with the orange zest, olive oil, and a generous pinch of salt. Toss to coat and marinate them for at least 30 minutes and up to 2 hours in the refrigerator.

Place the scallops on the grill adjacent to the coals of a medium fire (see page 15). Add some wood chips to the fire and cover the grill. (I prefer alder for scallops, but cherry, peach, and maple are equally good.) Close the air intake to a sliver and cook for 7 to 10 minutes, depending on the size of the scallops and intensity of the fire. I do not flip the scallops, as they cook fairly evenly. When cooked, they will be firm to the touch and shiny, with a trickle of exuded liquid. Serve them immediately.

Serves 4

Smoky Griddled Crab Cakes

Growing up near the Chesapeake Bay and spending a lot of time on its waters, I am a blue crab fanatic, born and bred. Its sweet flavor and meaty texture make for great crab cakes, but I have also had my fair share of bad crab cakes, too, mostly because chefs tried to get too fancy and complicated. If you start with great crab, the key to success is to just stay out of its way. So I was not looking to reinvent the crab cake one night when I had just finished grilling a couple of vegetable dishes and was heading to the stove to sear off the crab cakes for dinner. It struck me, why not cook the crab cakes, still in a cast-iron pan, over the grill? I spread out the coals and wood chunks and heated the heavy black pan directly over the coals. I added a little butter and cooked the cakes just as I would have done on my electric burners, but I covered the grill to capture some of the smoke. When the cakes were golden brown and crispy on both sides, I sat down to taste my experiment. And I loved them. The light smoke flavor was very flattering to the crab and was a fun new twist for an old favorite without dishonoring its tradition.

2 tablespoons mayonnaise

2 teaspoons Old Bay Seasoning

2 lemons, 1 juiced and the other cut into wedges for garnish

1 cup panko (Japanese-style bread crumbs)

1 pound jumbo lump Chesapeake (or from any domestic waters) crabmeat, picked through for cartilage

2 tablespoons unsalted butter

Mix the mayonnaise, Old Bay, lemon juice, and panko in a medium bowl and toss to combine. Add the crab and very gently mix with your hand until it binds together with the other ingredients. Form the mixture into four equal patties about 1½ inches thick. Refrigerate them for at least 20 minutes so the bread crumbs can absorb the moisture.

Heat a large cast-iron skillet directly over the coals of a medium fire (see page 15) flavored with apple wood. When the pan is hot, add the butter and rotate the pan until melted butter covers the bottom. Add the crab cakes and cook with the grill covered until they are golden brown and crispy, about 4 minutes per side. Serve hot with the lemon wedges.

Serves 4

Grilled Soft-Shell Crabs

When it comes to soft-shell crabs, the standard is to give them a light breading spiked with Old Bay Seasoning, then fry them until crisp in either a deep fryer or with butter in a sauté pan. But one day I popped a few of them over the coals, and I was impressed. In this method, no seasoning is needed; it yields a beautiful, crisp crab with a sweet sea aroma.

1 tablespoon canola oil

4 large soft-shell crabs, cleaned (ask your fishmonger to do this for you)

2 lemons, cut into wedges

Lightly oil the crabs, then place them on a grill, shell side down, directly over the coals of a medium fire (see page 15) flavored with oak, maple, or pecan wood. Cook until the edges of the shells begin to blacken, about 4 minutes. Rotate the grill grate so that the crabs are now away from the fire. Flip the crabs over and cover the grill. Cook for another 5 minutes.

Transfer the crabs to a platter and serve them immediately with the lemon wedges.

Serves 4

Grilled Calamari with Red Onion and Basil

I adore the pairing of basil and grilled squid. This combination is the foundation for a dish that I served in each of my restaurants, and it was always a top seller. This makes a great dish for entertaining, as the preparation is easy and the results are stunning.

1 pound cleaned calamari (ask your fishmonger a few days ahead for squid with the skin still on, known as dirty squid)

1 clove garlic, grated over a Microplane or very finely minced

Kosher salt

3 tablespoons extra-virgin olive oil

1 small red onion, thinly sliced vertically

Leaves from 4 sprigs fresh basil, torn

Mix together the squid, garlic, a pinch of salt, and 1 teaspoon of the olive oil. Toss to combine and let sit for at least 30 minutes and up to overnight in the refrigerator.

Right before grilling, mix the onion slices with 1 tablespoon of the olive oil and the torn basil. Season to taste with salt and gently toss to combine.

Place the squid on the grill directly over the coals of a medium fire (see page 15) flavored with your choice of fruitwood. Cook for 1 to 2 minutes and then flip. Cook until the squid is lightly caramelized and cooked through, about another 3 minutes. Be careful not to overcook.

Place the squid on serving plates and garnish with the onion mixture. Drizzle each plate with the remaining olive oil and serve immediately.

Serves 4

5 WINGS
chicken, turkey + duck

I find it funny that chicken is the epitome of comfort in our culture. When we are sick, we reach for its broth to soothe our souls. When we don't want to think about dinner, the default choice is chicken. When people are not courageous, we call them a chicken. And when we want to describe foods, we use chicken as a baseline flavor, as though chicken itself were the great common denominator of American food. I think that we are slightly chicken when it comes to thinking about chicken.

We have accepted tasteless factory-farmed chicken as normal. We covet price over quality—and are now paying for it. High-intensity factory farming is not a pretty sight. Turned into a commodity product, these animals are devalued, pushed through an inhumane system as fast as possible. No life is merely a product. All lives are part of an intricate system through which each can fulfill its needs as it supplies for the needs of others.

I don't want to be greedy here, but I really think that a chicken should taste like something. It's not so much to ask that it taste like chicken, is it?

By contrast, a wine tastes of everything experienced by the grapes it is made from— the sun that shone up on them, the wind, temperature, humidity, soil composition, etc. It is the sum of all of these things. The French call this terroir.

The terroir of most chickens these days is not something you would think could bring anything beautiful onto your plate. But if a chicken is allowed to act like a chicken, to run around in the grass pecking at bugs and rocks, the resulting product is bound to taste more like chicken. That seems fairly obvious. And during this chicken's life, it is part of a system, eating pests, spreading nutrients, providing eggs and, ultimately, meat. The chicken benefits from a life well lived, the farm is more efficient and prosperous, the pasture is richer for good soil and produces better forage. My good friend and visionary farmer Bev Eggleston convinced me of this years ago when I first started buying his birds for one of my signature dishes. "When we ask an animal to be our food, we must in turn give them the life they are supposed to live," he says.

When we as consumers do not participate in a natural system, we sacrifice quality and taste, and we rob the chicken of far more. You cannot remove the sun from a wine any more than you can remove the "life" from a chicken and still expect the same result. But this is exactly what we do.

When we cook, we express ourselves through hospitality and through our desire to nourish with more than calories. When I cook, I want ingredients that express themselves on the plate. Such ingredients can only come from a life in which the animal was allowed to express itself. We owe it at least that much.

This is the value that comes with connecting with the source of your food. This is why the food at farmers' markets often costs a little more, because you are getting more value. And this is the purpose of eating and of entertaining, to get the most from your food and to connect with friends and family.

Buy a chicken from a local farmer who practices humane farming techniques. Taste the difference, and don't be a chicken about discovering why there is a difference. We all have our own needs and our own motivations, which color our lives and drive our decisions. As Bev says, "All I ask is that you recognize that there is a difference and then decide if that matters to you."

Jerk Spice-Smoked Chicken Breast

This recipe borrows the provocative flavors of the classic Jamaican dish, a well-spiced method of cooking a host of different meats and seafood. The real key is the addition of allspice tree branches to the fire. These generate a deep and flavorful smoke. Not having access to these branches, I throw spices as well as wood chips into the fire to create an alluring and wildly different smoke flavor.

This is really a jerk-style reconstruction that combines the classic flavors at different points in the process, from brining to cooking.

2 cups warm water

1 cup orange juice

1½ tablespoons kosher salt

¼ cup firmly packed brown sugar

4 skin-on chicken breast halves with the wing bone attached (about 5 ounces each)

1 tablespoon extra-virgin olive oil

2 teaspoons ground mace

1 teaspoon cayenne pepper or ground chipotle chile

Freshly ground black pepper

2 tablespoons allspice berries

3 sticks cinnamon

6 sprigs fresh thyme

Combine the water, orange juice, salt, and brown sugar in a medium bowl and stir until dissolved. Submerge the chicken in the brine and refrigerate for 4 to 8 hours.

Remove the chicken from the brine and pat it dry. Rub the skin with the olive oil and season the skin side generously with the mace, chile, and pepper.

Sear the chicken, skin side down, just adjacent to the coals of a medium fire (see page 15). Do not move the breasts until you hear the skin begin to crackle and it turns crispy golden brown, 6 to 8 minutes, depending on the heat. Move the breasts to the cool side of the grill, turning them skin side up. Add a handful of maple or oak chips, half the allspice and cinnamon, and 3 sprigs thyme to the fire. You may need to rearrange the coals a little to form a base that will prevent the allspice berries from falling through. Cover the grill and cook for 5 minutes, then add the remaining spices and thyme to keep the flavorful smoke rolling. Grill until the breasts are cooked through, about another 5 minutes.

Remove the chicken breasts from the grill and let them rest for at least 5 minutes. I like to cut them into thin slices before serving, but that is up to you.

Serves 4

INGREDIENTS I LOVE: ALLSPICE

About the size of a peppercorn, this dried fruit of the allspice tree is a common ingredient in cuisines around the world. Given that its name comes from its rich aroma of clove, bay leaf, cinnamon, and anise, it can be a powerful addition to a dish. Its flavor can really be brought into focus by the addition of slight heat, such as cayenne pepper or a generous amount of freshly ground black pepper.

"Teriyaki" Chicken Salad

I put *teriyaki* in quotes because I have so little experience with Asian cuisines that I do not pretend to offer up an authentic interpretation of this sauce. I was taught something like this by a good friend of mine, and all I know is that it is absolutely delicious.

The dish takes cues from a Vietnamese salad of ground spiced chicken served with crispy vegetables and aromatic herbs. So this is a tasty mash-up of many different cuisines.

1 cup sugar

1 cup aji mirin (a sweet rice wine for cooking) or dry sack or amontillado sherry

½ cup white wine

1 cup soy sauce

1 lemon, cut in half

4 skinless, boneless chicken breast halves (about 4 ounces each)

1 large red onion, sliced as thinly as possible into half moons

6 stalks celery, sliced as thinly as possible

Leaves from 1 bunch fresh mint, roughly chopped

2 tablespoons Chile-Infused Oil (page 271) or extra-virgin olive oil

Combine the sugar, mirin, wine, and soy sauce in a medium saucepan. Simmer over medium heat until reduced by half. Remove from the heat, add the lemon halves (don't squeeze the juice out of them), and steep for 15 minutes. Remove and discard the lemon halves. Let the marinade cool.

Place the chicken in an 8-inch square glass baking dish or zip-top plastic bag and pour in half of the marinade. Cover or seal the dish and marinate in the refrigerator for at least 4 hours and up to 2 days.

Make a medium fire in a grill (see page 15) and add a hearty wood such as hickory or mesquite. When the wood has burned to embers, place the chicken on the grill grate away from the fire. Cover the grill and cook until the chicken is cooked through and an instant-read thermometer reads 160 degrees F when inserted into the thickest part of each breast, 12 to 15 minutes. Take the chicken off the grill and let rest while you put together the salad.

In a medium bowl, toss together the onion, celery, mint, and chile oil. Divide the salad among the dinner plates. Slice each chicken breast as thinly as possible and arrange it over the salad on each plate. Drizzle the reserved "teriyaki" over the plates and serve immediately.

Serves 4

Rosemary-Skewered Chicken and Vegetable Kebabs

There is something about kebabs that makes good cooks lose their good sense. A chunk of meat is threaded on, then a piece of pepper, onion, tomato, and mushroom, then protein again and then repeat. The problem? Cherry tomatoes do not cook at the same pace as chicken. Nor do mushrooms cook with the same speed as peppers. The solution? Give each ingredient its own skewer, simple as that. And please don't crowd them together, or you prevent the heat from penetrating the food evenly.

1 pound boneless, skinless chicken thighs, cut into 1-inch pieces

12 stalks fresh rosemary, each about 12 inches long

2 red or yellow bell peppers, cut lengthwise into quarters and seeded

1 pint cherry tomatoes

1 pound pearl onions, peeled but left whole

3 tablespoons extra-virgin olive oil

1 tablespoon kosher salt

2 teaspoons dried oregano

1 tablespoon sherry vinegar

Make a medium fire in the grill (see page 15); when it burns down to coals, add your choice of fruitwood chips or chunks.

Using a metal or bamboo skewer, puncture a hole in the chicken chunks and thread them onto the rosemary stalks through the same hole. Do the same with the remaining vegetables, threading all that you can onto each rosemary stalk.

When all the chicken and vegetables have been skewered, drizzle them with the olive oil and season with the salt and oregano.

Place the chicken skewers just adjacent to the coals of the fire and the onion skewers just behind the chicken on the far side, away from the fire. Cover the grill and cook for 10 minutes.

Place the pepper skewers directly over the coals and cook until they are well charred and the skins have blistered. Remove the peppers to the far side of the grill. Flip the chicken and onion skewers. Place the tomatoes over the coals and cook until they begin to burst with the heat, 3 to 5 minutes. Remove the tomatoes, peppers, and onions from the grill.

Check to ensure that the chicken is cooked through; an instant-read thermometer inserted into the center of the chunks should read 160 degrees F. Remove the chicken from the grill and serve it immediately, with the vegetables still on the rosemary stalks, sprinkle the whole plate with sherry vinegar, allowing your guests to remove what they would like to their plates. This has the benefit of transferring the charred rosemary flavor to your guests' hands, enhancing their enjoyment of the dish even more!

Serves 4

Grilled Chicken Wings

Traditionally, wings are bathed in a hot sauce that is too spicy to really taste anything. But that just strengthens my suspicion that wings are just a socially acceptable way of shoveling blue cheese dressing into your mouth. Here's my take on the matter: a recipe should accentuate the great flavor of the chicken, not hide it. And blue cheese dressing is not necessary, due to the rich smoke flavor and bright acidity from the brine—but a little hot sauce wouldn't hurt.

2 tablespoons kosher salt

2 tablespoons molasses

2 tablespoons cider vinegar

1 cup water

2 pounds chicken wings

Combine all the ingredients in a large bowl and stir well. Let the wings marinate in the refrigerator for 8 hours, then drain but do not pat them dry.

Place the wings on the grill adjacent to the coals of a small fire (see page 15). Mesquite is the best wood for this, so add a few chunks to the coals, cover the grill, and choke the airflow by half. Cook for 10 minutes, then check the wings. They should be a deep caramel color. Move the wings directly over the coals, skin side down, and cook them for about 2 minutes to crisp the skin.

Serve the wings immediately. If desired, offer your guests some homemade Mezcal Hot Sauce (see page 277) or a bottle of hot sauce such as Tapatío or Frank's Red Hot. Oh, and give them lots of napkins.

Serves 4

Chicken Legs with Cilantro and Yogurt Marinade

Chicken legs are my favorite part of the bird—well, thighs actually. The dark meat is so much more flavorful and easier to cook, because it does not dry out nearly as fast as the white meat of the breasts does. The yogurt marinade is similar to that used in Indian tandoori recipes. It forms an intense and tangy crust on the outside of the meat, leaving the inside moist and well flavored. I like the addition of cilantro to this, but if you're not fond of it, mint works equally well.

1 tablespoon kosher salt

Juice of 1 lemon

2 tablespoons extra-virgin olive oil

3 tablespoons plain Greek-style yogurt

1 cup picked fresh cilantro leaves, half chopped and half left whole

4 skin-on whole chicken legs (thighs included)

In a large bowl, combine the salt, lemon juice, olive oil, yogurt, and chopped cilantro. Stir to combine, then add the chicken. Turn the legs in the mixture to thoroughly coat them. Marinate in the refrigerator for at least 1 hour and up to a day; the chicken only gets better as it sits.

Place the legs, skin side down, just adjacent to the coals of a medium fire (see page 15) flavored with citrus or apricot wood. Cover the grill and cook until the skin begins to char, about 5 minutes. Remove the legs to the cooler side of the grill and pour any remaining marinade over them. Cover the grill and cook until the meat is uniform in color, pulls easily away from the bone, and shows no pink color, about 20 minutes.

Transfer the chicken to a platter. Garnish it with the whole cilantro leaves and serve immediately.

Serves 4

Peruvian Chicken

I grew up in a largely immigrant neighborhood in DC that was well served by a host of restaurants dishing out the flavors of home for many of these newly American families. Among my lasting favorites are the Peruvian chicken places, always there to welcome you with a slightly greasy cloud of delicious chicken scent as you walk through the door. The secret to this chicken is the marinade and a slow turn in a rotisserie oven.

When you grill at home, this can be replicated with whole birds that have been bathed in marinade for a day, or with your choice of pieces given just a few hours to swim in this heady mix. The key to the marinade is the acid, provided by fresh lime juice and a touch of vinegar; it really penetrates the meat and carries the flavors of the spices through to great effect.

Juice of 2 limes

2 tablespoons white wine vinegar

1 tablespoon kosher salt

1 tablespoon granulated sugar

2 teaspoons extra-virgin olive oil

1 teaspoon ground cumin

2 teaspoons smoked sweet paprika

2 teaspoons powdered chile pepper, such as Espelette (page 55) or merquén (from Chile)

4 skin-on whole chicken legs (thighs included)

In a large glass baking dish, mix the lime juice, vinegar, salt and sugar. Stir to dissolve. Combine the olive oil, cumin, paprika, and chile pepper in a small pan and heat over medium heat until the spices are aromatic and the oil begins to bubble, about 3 minutes. Add this hot oil mixture to the lime juice mixture. Let cool, then add the chicken pieces, turning to coat them with the marinade. Cover and refrigerate for at least 4 hours and preferably overnight. Let the chicken come to room temperature before cooking it; this requires about 30 minutes out of the refrigerator.

Build a medium fire in a grill (see page 15) and add chunks of a flavorful wood such as maple, oak, or hickory. When the wood has burned down to embers, place the chicken, skin side down, directly over the coals. Cook for 2 minutes, then rotate the grill grate so the chicken is away from the fire. Cover the grill and cook until an instant-read thermometer registers 160 degrees F when inserted along the leg bone, about 20 minutes.

Transfer the chicken to a platter and serve immediately.

Serves 4

Grill-Braised Chicken with Preserved Lemon and Olives

Braising over a grill is a tricky undertaking, but the resulting dish more than makes up for the attention to detail necessary to pull it off. In this dish the simple and homely chicken thigh is slowly seduced into aromatic tenderness by a sultry mix of bay leaf, olives, preserved lemons, and the smoky undertones of the fire.

2 tablespoons extra-virgin olive oil

1 small onion, cut into large dice

2 cloves garlic, peeled

2 bay leaves

4 skin-on whole chicken legs (thighs included)

½ cup whole green olives (I prefer Manzanilla or picholine)

2 wedges Preserved Lemons (page 282), flesh cut away and discarded, peel cut into thin strips

2 cups dry white wine

2 sprigs fresh tarragon

Kosher salt to taste

Build a medium fire in your grill (see page 15) and let it burn until it is reduced to coals. Add wood chunks, preferably a soft-flavored wood such as peach or pecan. Place a heavy flameproof braising pan directly over the fire. Add the olive oil, onion, garlic, and bay leaves. Cook for a few minutes, until the onion begins to soften. Add the chicken and remaining ingredients. Heat until the wine is just below a boil.

Add a cup or two of warm water to cover the chicken thighs. You may need to rearrange the contents so that the chicken is submerged. Move the pan to the cooler side of the grill and cover the grill. Depending on the intensity of the fire, the chicken should be cooked through in about 1½ hours. If you have a thermometer on your grill or an oven thermometer you can steal, the temperature you are trying to maintain is between 275 and 325 degrees F. Check every 20 minutes or so to ensure that there is sufficient heat to continue the cooking; if necessary, add a few more wood chunks and cover the grill again. The key to this dish is that the dying fire captured within the closed grill provides a consistent, flavorful heat that slowly cooks the chicken. When the meat is done, it should be tender, flaking off the bone with gentle pressure.

Once the chicken is cooked, it can be served immediately or, even better, you can chill the whole pan, then gently reheat it over low heat on the stove and serve it the next day.

Serves 4

Black Pepper and Honey Chicken

There are a couple of really great Chinese restaurants in DC that cater to a late-night crowd. When you get off work in the kitchens at one or two A.M. and are desperately hungry, there are few options. Go to one of these restaurants in the wee hours, and you're guaranteed to see bleary-eyed cooks and chefs sitting down to a long-overdue meal. After everyone else has been fed, the cooks deserve to eat too!

One of the real eye-opening things about these late-night meals is that the Chinese cooks have a willing audience ready to explore the true tastes of the cuisine. Chinese food is not just sweet and salty. Give these chefs a chance to cook as they do for their families, and there are revelations to be experienced. One of the best is the use of spicy and sour to balance a dish. The other is sweet and spicy—the gentle heat of chiles spiriting the light sweetness into a perfect partnership.

This dish is inspired by the late-night meals I have shared with my weary colleagues. Do not skimp on the pepper. It is supposed to pack a punch, and if you so desire, a pinch or two of cayenne is a nice addition.

2 tablespoons coarse-ground Dijon mustard

2 tablespoons honey

Juice of 2 limes or lemons

1 tablespoon kosher salt

A good amount of fresh coarsely ground black pepper

One 3- to 4-pound chicken, split in half

Combine the mustard, honey, citrus juice, and salt in a large glass baking dish. Add a generous grinding of black pepper. Place the chicken halves in the dish and turn to coat well with the mixture. Cover and refrigerate for at least 12 hours and up to 2 days. Let the chicken come to room temperature before cooking; this requires about 30 minutes out of the refrigerator.

Build a medium fire in the grill (page 15) and add chunks of the fruitwood of your choice. When the wood has burned to embers, place the chicken halves, skin side down, just adjacent to the coals. Cover the grill and cook for 10 minutes.

Flip the chicken halves so that the bone and cavity are facing down. Brush on any remaining marinade, cover the grill, and close the air vents to a sliver. Cook until an instant-read thermometer registers 160 degrees F when placed against the leg bone, about 20 minutes. Remove from the grill, let rest for 5 minutes, then separate the legs from the breasts, and serve immediately.

Serves 4

Grill-Roasted Chicken

Smaller birds are easier to manage on the grill in terms of ensuring doneness, plus I like serving a half bird to each guest. The brine is an important component of this recipe and replaces the need to season the birds before cooking. Drizzling the chickens with lemon-infused oil for the last few minutes of cooking adds an incredible scent that really enlivens the meat.

The choice of wood for this is key, as too strong a flavor will mask the delicate nature of a pasture-raised bird. Will it taste good if heavily smoked with mesquite or hickory? Sure it will. But it won't taste much like chicken. I have recently come to really appreciate the smoky flavor citrus wood generates. Another delicious option is to make a wood fire of oak or maple, in which the wood is providing more heat than aromatic smoke, then add dried fennel stalks above the grate so that they smolder alongside the chicken. Or add the dried stalks of end-of-the-season basil plants. They impart a wonderful musky basil flavor that is perfect with chicken, though the smoke they generate can sometimes smell like the parking lot at a Grateful Dead concert.

Two 2-pound young chickens, or one 3½- to 4-pound bird

2 recipes Poultry Brine (page 262)

3 tablespoons brightly flavored olive oil (I greatly prefer Meyer lemon-infused olive oil, see Infused Oils, page 273)

Place the chickens in a large bowl or pot and pour in the brine. Cover and refrigerate for 12 to 24 hours.

Drain the brine. Place the chickens on a baking sheet and dry them with a desk fan for an hour to form a tacky layer on the skin surface; this is called a pellicle, and it's what the smoke flavor will stick to. You can also dry them overnight, uncovered, in the refrigerator.

Build a large fire in the grill (page 15). When it has died down to embers, add the flavoring wood chips or stalks. Place the chickens on the grill away from the coals, with the legs closer to the fire. Cover the grill and choke the airflow to a sliver. Cook for 30 minutes, adding more wood chips if necessary to keep a billowing smoke going. Check the birds with an instant-read thermometer inserted into the leg against the bone. It should register between 135 and 140 degrees F. Rotate the birds so that the breasts are closest to the fire. Cover the grill and cook for another 10 minutes. Uncover the grill and drizzle the birds with 1 tablespoon of the olive oil, then cover and cook until the thermometer registers 160 degrees F, about another 5 minutes.

Remove the birds from the grill and let them rest for 15 minutes. Section the birds into legs and breasts and drizzle them with the remaining 2 tablespoons olive oil. Serve immediately.

Serves 4 to 6

Smoked Turkey

There has been a Thanksgiving trend recently toward the deep-fried turkey, a dangerous method with questionable merit. But have you ever thought about smoking your bird? Picture it: you, not a bead of sweat on your brow, emerging to the gloriously set table through the swinging kitchen door, back first to the assembled adoring family and then gracefully, a half pirouette, to reveal the deeply caramel colored bird, flecked with a scented confetti of orange zest, the savory aroma silencing the room as you proudly settle the dish into its ceremonial spot.

1 heritage turkey (10 to 12 pounds)

4 recipes Poultry Brine made with cranberry juice (page 262)

Grated zest and juice of 1 orange

2 tablespoons extra-virgin olive oil

8 allspice berries, ground in a mortar

Place the turkey in a very large bowl or pot and pour the brine in to cover it. Cover and refrigerate for 24 to 36 hours.

Drain the brine. Place the turkey on a baking sheet, pat dry, and let sit, uncovered, in the refrigerator for 12 hours, or put it on the counter and turn a desk fan on it for an hour or two. This will help to make a tacky layer on the surface called a pellicle, which is what the smoke will adhere to.

Build a medium fire in a smoker or large grill (see page 15) and let it burn to coals. Place a flameproof pan filled with water in the smoker, then the turkey on the rack above it. If using a grill, place the pan of water directly over the coals on the grill grate. Add a number of chunks of lightly aromatic wood such as alder or apple or another fruitwood. Close the smoker or grill and monitor the temperature using a built-in thermometer or an oven thermometer. It should be between 200 and 250 degrees F, but no higher. Continue to add wood chunks as necessary to maintain billowing smoke and a consistent temperature.

After smoking for 2 hours, mix the orange juice and zest, olive oil, and ground allspice together in a small bowl. Baste the turkey with the mixture every half hour for the next 2 hours as the bird continues to smoke. After 4 hours of smoking, remove the bird from the smoker and test the internal temperature of the leg just against the bone with an instant-read thermometer. It should read between 135 and 150 degrees F. If it registers 150 degrees F, skip the next step and head straight to the broiler.

Transfer the turkey to a roasting pan and place it in a preheated 300-degree F oven. Cook for another 20 minutes, until a thermometer inserted into the thigh registers just under 150 degrees F.

Switch the oven to broil and cook for 10 minutes to super-crisp the skin. If your bird was already 150 degrees F or higher coming out of the grill, broil it for just a few minutes. Remove the turkey from the oven, let it rest for at least 25 minutes, then make your grand entrance!

Serves up to 10 people (given a good quantity of side dishes)

Cornish Hen Grilled "Under Brick"

This is my take on a classic Tuscan preparation of chicken called *pollo al mattone,* which means "chicken cooked under a brick." The technique is a wonderful way to produce a super crispy skin and moist, tender meat throughout. In this recipe, I use lots of fresh herbs to add flavor to the bird while it marinates and when it cooks; on the grill, the herbs char and become a delicious crust.

The key to this dish is the weight applied to the bird. You can use a foil-wrapped brick, a heavy cast-iron pan, a pan of water, whatever won't burn as it presses the bird to the flame.

Two 1½-pound Cornish hens, butterflied

1 recipe Herb Marinade (page 269)

Kosher salt

Place the hens in a deep-sided baking dish, add the marinade, and season them generously with salt. Turn to coat them evenly and let them marinate in the refrigerator at least an hour but preferably overnight.

Place the birds, skin side down, on the grill directly over the coals of a small fire (page 15) flavored with any kind of fruitwood. Place a foil-wrapped brick or heavy cast iron pan directly on top of the birds. Cook for about 2 minutes, then rotate the grate so the birds are away from the coals. Cover the grill and cook for 20 to 25 minutes. Check the doneness of the birds by removing the brick and gently slicing between the leg and the thigh. If the flesh is opaque and the juices run clear, then remove the birds from the fire. If they need to cook longer, add a few wood chunks to the fire and cover the grill. Check every 5 minutes until they are cooked through.

Transfer the birds to a cutting board and let them rest for at least 10 minutes before cutting them in half and serving.

Serves 4

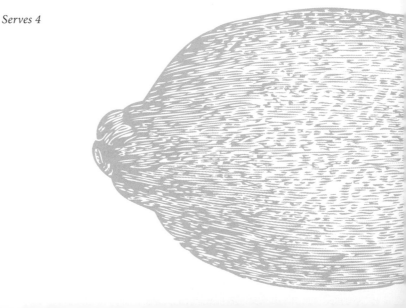

Grilled Quail in Guinness Marinade

Quail make a really great centerpiece for an outdoor meal. They are expensive, but you really don't need more than one, maybe two per person. The slight gamy flavor of the meat is complemented well by dark Guinness stout. When buying quail, always get semiboneless. Full bone-in quail are not fun to eat, as it's difficult to get at all the meat.

4 to 8 semiboneless quail (depends on your crowd, but I think one is enough per person)

1 recipe Guinness Marinade (page 268)

Kosher salt

1 tablespoon Chile-Infused Oil (page 271) or Basil Oil (page 270)

Leaves from 3 sprigs fresh cilantro (if using Chile-Infused Oil), torn

Place the quail in a large baking dish and pour the marinade over them. Cover and marinate the quail in the refrigerator for at least 4 hours and up to a day.

Remove the birds from the marinade and discard the liquid. Season them lightly with salt and set them on the grill, breast side down, just adjacent to the coals of a small fire (see page 15) to which you've added a small amount of a heavily flavored wood such as hickory or mesquite. Cook with the grill covered until the skin begins to crisp, 3 to 4 minutes. Flip the birds, move them to the coolest part of the grill, and cover them again. Cook for another 3 minutes, then transfer them to a platter. These birds cook very quickly, but to ensure that they are done, gently pry one leg away from the bird. The exposed meat should be grayish in color, with just a hint of pink.

Drizzle the flavored oil over the birds. If you're using the chile oil, scatter the cilantro over the birds and serve them immediately. If you use basil oil, no herb garnish is needed.

Serves 4

Crispy-Skin Grilled Duck Confit

Traditionally, duck was turned into confit as a way to preserve it; the salted and slowly cooked legs covered in a thick layer of their own fat would keep for many months. Like many dishes born of rural efficiency, confit is now rarely found outside of high-end restaurants. If you haven't ever tried duck confit, you need to—it is incredible in a way you can't even imagine. Though I provide a from-scratch recipe, the good news is that you can buy already prepared confit that is very good; my favorite is that made by D'Artagnan. Whether you make or buy your confit, the fatty legs and meltingly tender meat are greatly enhanced once you crisp the skin over a smoky fire and serve the dish with a salad of crisp endive and aromatic herbs.

6 fresh duck legs

3 tablespoons kosher salt

1 tablespoon brown sugar

Leaves from 3 sprigs fresh thyme

Freshly ground black pepper

4 to 6 cups canola oil or rendered duck fat

6 heads Belgian endive, ends trimmed and leaves separated

Leaves from ½ bunch fresh flat-leaf parsley

1 cup fennel or dill fronds

Juice of 1 lemon

Wash the duck legs under cold running water and pat them dry. Combine the salt, brown sugar, thyme, and 3 or 4 turns of pepper. Sprinkle about 1 tablespoon of the salt mix in a large baking dish and lay the legs, skin side up, in the dish. Cover the legs with the remaining salt mix. Cover and refrigerate for 2 days.

Brush off the remaining cure mix and transfer the legs to a pan just big enough to hold them snugly. Cover the duck with the oil, put a lid on the pan, and cook over low to medium heat (you want to maintain a very low temperature, just enough to cause gentle and infrequent bubbling) until the meat is falling-off-the-bone tender, about 3 hours. Let cool to room temperature, then refrigerate overnight. If you are planning on storing the confit for an extended period, remove the legs and separate the fat from any cooking liquid that has collected in the bottom of the pan. Completely cover the legs with the fat, and they will keep in the refrigerator for a couple of months.

When you're ready to grill, remove the duck legs from the fat (or from the package, if you're using store-bought) and wipe them clean of any excess fat. Place the legs on the grill away from the coals of a small fire (see page 15) and cover. (This will heat the legs through and melt away any remaining fat, which will prevent a grease fire when you sear them later directly over the coals.) I really like to use citrus wood to season the fire when making this recipe, but any fruitwood is fine. When the legs are heated all the way through, about 15 minutes, move them directly over the coals and cook until the skin is darkly caramelized and crispy, about 3 minutes. If the fire begins to flare, remove the duck immediately, wipe away any fat from the legs, and try cooking them adjacent to the fire for a longer time.

To serve, mix the endive, parsley, and fennel with the lemon juice and toss to combine. This salad needs no fat or salt (the duck has enough of both, I promise). Divide the salad among the plates and lay one leg on top. Serve immediately.

Makes 6 servings

Smoked Duck Breast with Orange and Coriander

Here I use the classic combination of orange and coriander but round it out with the addition of brown sugar, which slowly caramelizes and absorbs the smoky character of the fire as it heats on the grill. The orange, still assertive, cuts through the sweetness of the sugar and rich fatness of the duck.

This is a very hearty dish, so I prefer to serve a smaller portion. You can easily double the recipe should you care for a more substantial amount.

2 skin-on duck breasts (about 8 ounces each)

Finely shredded zest and juice of 1 orange

2 tablespoons light brown sugar

2 teaspoons ground coriander

1 tablespoon kosher salt

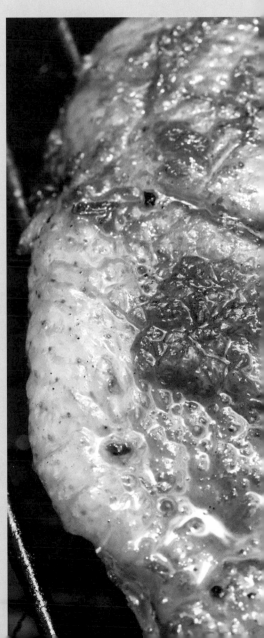

Wash the duck breasts under cold running water and pat them dry. Score the fat side with a sharp knife, making shallow incisions in a crosshatch pattern. Do not cut through the fat down to the meat.

In a small bowl, mix the orange zest and juice, brown sugar, coriander, and salt until well combined. Spread the spice mix evenly over the fat side of the duck and let marinate for up to an hour at room temperature or up to overnight in the refrigerator.

Place the duck breasts, fat side up, on the grill away from the coals of a small fire (see page 15), add a few wood chunks (I prefer a fruitwood for this) to the fire, and cover the grill. Cook over low heat for 20 minutes or so. Lift the cover and check the doneness of the duck. It should be about medium rare at this point. If this is to your liking (I recommend medium rare to medium), remove the duck from the grill and let it rest for at least 10 minutes. For greater degrees of doneness, I suggest an extra 3 minutes per level.

If you wish, place the breasts, fat side up, under a preheated broiler for just 1 or 2 minutes to crisp the surface. While I enjoy this crisp texture, I prefer the fat to retain the super luscious quality it has when served straight from the grill.

Slice the duck as thinly as possibly on a slight bias and serve immediately.

Serves 4

6 HOOVES
beef, pork + lamb

There is a great debate in our country about the meat we eat: the quantity consumed, its provenance, and the health of the animals and of ourselves as a result of our meals. I am thankful for this discussion, as it is long overdue. The science of agriculture is at once both a blessing and a distraction. We are fortunate to have so much food and to be able to feed so many billions. But it also moves us away from an acknowledgment that we are a part of the agricultural system.

As technology has advanced, it has divided the interconnected structure of farming into component parts. What had always been a responsive and diversified system has become a factory that relies on uniformity to achieve its overarching goal of efficiency. This never-ending drive for economy has led to amazing things. But we have allowed some valuable ideals to be left behind in its wake.

Most important, we have forgotten about the animal in this equation. By focusing only on meat, we have lost compassion for the creature that gives its life so that we may eat. When we fail to recognize the source of our food, we fail to embrace its purpose in our lives. Food connects each of us to a rich internal account of memories and experiences. We identify ourselves through food, and the choices that we make at the dinner table define the culture in agriculture.

If, as the saying goes, "you are what you eat," what does that make us if we eat meat from an animal that never knew compassion? In every community, there are farmers who treat animals with care and compassion, who allow (and expect) animals to behave as they should—a cow foraging through pastures in search of sweet clover, a sow wallowing in the sun. These farmers produce the best-quality meat and provide us with an opportunity to invest in our local economies and in our own health.

Good meat is an investment of money, too. It is not cheap. But it's also important to acknowledge the value we gain beyond calories. Many of the environmental costs of meat disappear when compassion is introduced, and efficiencies appear elsewhere on the farm that drive the cost of other goods down.

With each bite, we must savor and appreciate our place in the systems of this world. And that's not so hard to do when good-quality meat has been carefully roasted over a slow and soulful fire, brought to the table with respectful ceremony, and appropriately apportioned. Seek flavor—deep flavor that can only come from acknowledging what is given to us. Just as a meal tastes better after a hard day's work, so too does flavor soar when we recognize the total ecosystem by which we gain our daily bread. When we acknowledge our place in these systems, our palates and our bodies will reap the rewards.

A Griller's Guide to Meat

Beef

When grilling beefsteaks, checking the internal temperature using an instant-read thermometer is your best bet for determining whether they've reached the preferred doneness: 125 degrees F for rare; 130 to 135 degrees F, medium rare; 135 to 140 degrees F, medium; 145 to 150 degrees F, medium well; and 155 degrees F, well done. I cook my steaks to medium rare, as I find that results in the best texture while also giving the beef just enough time to take on the flavors of the grill.

Strip loin steak

This cut comes from the spine of the animal and connects to the rib eye just before the thirteenth rib. Toward the rib end, these steaks have better marbling and, in my opinion, are more tender. As the strip continues toward the tail, it becomes leaner, and develops a narrow band of sinew toward the sirloin end that separates the top third of the steak. Ask your butcher for cuts from the center or rib end, or ask for a lower price on the sirloin end cuts. Also known as New York strip, Kansas City strip, strip steak, or hotel steak.

Tip: Many people consider the strip to be the best steak for grilling. It has a finely grained texture and can be quite dense, so it can take a sear well and it has a bit of a chew. I like this slight bite, and the flavor more than makes up for it. Because the steak is quite lean and can dry out, it needs to be cooked with care. I like cooking one large, very thick steak to serve many people, as it helps to best take advantage of its unique qualities.

Rib steak

These are taken from the center of the rib area between the sixth and twelfth ribs. The muscle here is very well marbled and has a wonderful texture, soft and yielding but with a pleasant chew. The steaks can be a little fragile, as they sometimes have a nugget of fat separating the muscle toward the shoulder end, and the grain of the meat is quite soft, almost porous. The steaks toward the back end of the animal are leaner and more consistent. Also known as rib eye when boneless and sometimes referred to as a Delmonico.

Tip: This is my favorite cut of beef to grill. I think it has the best flavor-to-texture balance. This is not a steak to fiddle with once it's on the grill, as every touch can exacerbate its fragility; in the worst case, the steak can pull apart. But it is the "porous" texture of the meat that makes it so great on the grill. Fat absorbs smoke well, but so does the meat in this cut; even lean grass-fed rib steaks will take on smoke well.

Tenderloin

Considered the most elegant of all the cuts. This is the tenderest part of the animal, as it is a minor muscle that rests along the inner spine. The tenderloin does not have a whole lot of flavor or fat. Many chefs dismiss the cut for this reason, opting instead for the more robust taste found elsewhere on the animal. Tenderloin steaks are referred to as tournedos or filet mignon. And when the thickest part of the tenderloin is served as a cut for two, it may be called Chateaubriand.

Tip: These steaks should be perfectly trimmed of fat and sinew before grilling. I prefer to cook a large portion of this cut, as it allows for more time on the grill to absorb flavor; then I chill it and slice it super-thin.

T-bone steak

This is a bone-in cut that includes the strip steak and, on the opposite side of the bone, a small portion of tenderloin.

Tip: Cooking a T-bone can be a little challenging, due to the fact that it is composed of two different muscles, each cooking at a different pace. This can be mitigated by slowly roasting the steaks until they're done to the desired internal temperature and then searing them directly over the fire just before removing. Also, please see page 244 for tips on how to cook a steak with the bone in.

Porterhouse steak

The same as a T-bone but with a larger portion of tenderloin.

Tip: The porterhouse faces the same cooking challenges as the T-bone. See above.

Hanger steak

Once coveted by butchers and kept for their own enjoyment, this steak has recently become quite the darling of restaurant chefs. The cut comes from the area called the plate, just behind the front legs on the underside of the animal. It is attached to part of the diaphragm and is associated with the outer skirt steak. The area is not part of the four primal portions of the animal and so is sold separately as part of the so-called "fifth quarter" or "hanging cuts." This muscle is not particularly tender, but it has great flavor and an enjoyable chew. When using the hanger, it is very important to find the grain of the meat and to slice across it, or it will be unyielding and tough. Also known as the onglet or bistro steak.

Tip: This is a great steak for dishes such as fajitas or tacos, as the meat packs such big flavor that even super-thin slices can carry a dish. I like to cook this steak quickly, because I have always found it to get tough when left for longer times over low heat. These steaks are lean and not very thick, but they can develop a nice charred crust while maintaining a red center. I do not recommend cooking them past medium.

Flank steak

Another one of the "hanging cuts," this comes from the underbelly of the animal. The flank is a thin, flat round muscle that is very flavorful and has a wonderfully chewy texture.

Tip: Flank steak takes marinades well and has its own hearty flavor to match. It is similar in cooking to hanger and skirt steaks. Flank should not be cooked past medium, or it will dry out completely. It is a very lean cut and should be cooked fairly quickly. This makes a wonderful cut for cold salads, because the meat has a pleasant texture when chilled.

Skirt steak

This cut refers to two different muscles, the outside skirt and the inside skirt. The outside is a muscle that is part of the diaphragm, and the inside is part of the flank, the underbelly near the rear legs. Both muscles are covered in a tough membrane that must be removed before cooking. The outside skirt can be quite chewy but has good flavor, while the inside is prized for its tenderness and flavor.

Tip: Both types of skirt steak are much like the flank and hanger in terms of cooking technique. They cook very quickly, so a hot fire is a necessity. Both take marinades well, especially if there is a little sugar in the mix, as it will promote a nice charred crust to give a textural contrast to the pleasantly chewy meat.

Tri-tip

This is one of the muscles that make up the bottom sirloin. When removed from the sirloin and cooked on its own, it has a wonderful texture and a grainy, flavorful bite. They are usually about 2 pounds apiece and make for a great party cut.

Tip: Tri-tip can be grilled whole, my preference, or cut into steaks. This cut is delicious when served at room temperature or chilled, which makes for easy entertaining because it can be cooked before guests arrive.

Blade

This steak comes from the complicated jumble of muscles that is the shoulder. The muscle known as the top blade is one of the tenderest in the shoulder, and it has an amazing depth of flavor. A vein of tough sinew runs through the middle, but its effect can be minimized through proper cutting before and after cooking. Also known as a flatiron steak.

Tip: This can be portioned into steaks or grill-roasted whole and then sliced very thin. I like to butterfly the steak to remove the sinew, then stuff it with hot ratatouille, roll it up, tie it, and roast it on the grill. Using hot stuffing helps to ensure even, and much quicker, cooking.

Top sirloin

This is one of the leanest cuts of tender beef. It has a good chew and a deep, meaty flavor.

Tip: I don't particularly love this steak for eating just off the grill, but it comes into its own when slowly grilled, then chilled and sliced for salad.

Short ribs

This is usually considered a braising cut in American cuisine. It is wonderful on the grill, though, as when it is sliced thin across the bone for the Korean dish kalbi. This cut can be a joy to eat and just a very small portion is enough to satisfy. This is about as fatty I like beef to be.

Tip: The short rib can be cooked both on the bone or off. The meat is chewy when grilled, but pleasantly so. Leaving the bone in can increase this characteristic chew, but it also provides a welcome and tasty utensil with which to eat the meat. Short ribs are thirsty for smoke flavor and will absorb quite a lot, so a gentle-flavored wood is best. The ribs also stand up well to spicy seasonings and rich BBQ sauces.

Brisket

This is another "hanging cut." The meat is legendary in many cuisines, from Jewish holiday feasts, to the corned beef of Ireland, to Texas Hill Country BBQ. It comes from the front of the animal on what we would consider the chest area between the two front legs. It has a thick fat cap known as the deckle, which should be left on for preparations like corned beef (in my opinion), but when going to the grill, it is best to remove it so as to prevent flare-ups. Brisket needs to cook for many hours to soften the dense and fibrous meat, so plan ahead.

Tip: This cut is the true test of a Texas barbecue cook. While pork is the chosen meat in the East and South, Texans slow-smoke beef briskets for many hours, yielding a super-tender and richly flavored sliced meat. Brisket does not work for short cooking times and is, therefore, not used for grilling, but ground up for burgers, it makes for some tasty eating. I like to braise brisket in a mixture of red wine and aromatic vegetables, cool it overnight in its broth, and then reheat it slowly on a smoky grill before serving it with a reduction of the braising liquid.

Pork

I like pork cooked with a hint of pink in the center, what would be called medium well in beef but is considered medium for pork, 135 to 140 degrees F. Don't serve it under medium; the texture is slippery and squeaky and just not very good. At the other end of the range, overly done pork should be avoided, as it is dry and tasteless.

Tenderloin

Pork tenderloin is from the back side of the loin. While pork loin is sometimes cut into T-bone style chops, it is much more common to see the tenderloin sold separately. Tenderloin is rarely cut into portions, as they usually weigh only 1 to 2 pounds apiece. This cut is very tender and very lean, with mild flavor. Because it is has little or no fat, tenderloin can dry out easily.

Tip: These are perfect on the grill, as a whole tenderloin will serve a party of four or more in grand fashion. Brining and a well-spiced seasoning help to make the most of this cut, and slow grilling is the best way to preserve moisture and flavor. Let it rest for at least 15 minutes before slicing it super-thin.

Loin and chops

What are commonly referred to as pork chops can vary quite a bit depending on the part of the animal they come from. Toward the shoulder, the chops have several veins of thick fat running through them; this disappears further toward the hind, and the loin becomes less marbled and more consistent in shape and size.

Tip: While I prefer the flavor and fat of the shoulder end, the center cuts from the loin are most commonly found in stores. I prefer to cook chops with the bone in for the contrast of the rib meat along the "handle" of the bone with the lean and moist loin meat. Pork fat has a pleasant texture and crisps well as it cooks. For that reason, I leave more fat on pork chops than I do on beef steaks, but I also don't eat them very often. All pork heading for the grill is greatly improved by a preliminary soak in brine (see page 263).

Shoulder

Most chefs would probably pick this as their desert-island protein (I would choose fish, given that I would be on an island). The shoulder is incredibly versatile and is the basis of most charcuterie products. It comprises a number of different muscles and so can be difficult to navigate with a knife. But this is the most forgiving meat there is, due to its high fat content and relatively tender meat.

Tip: This is the cut of pork used for slow-cooked barbecue, your classic pulled pork. While it does exceptionally well in long, slow cooking, it is equally delicious as a quick grill cut. It can be cut into broad slices, with or without the bone, and crisped directly over the fire. Be careful, though, as it has a lot of fat, which will drip and burn. So sear it very quickly, then roast it away from the flames for an easy cross between a chop and the smoky, moist barbecue style.

Ribs

There are many different parts of the rib that go to culinary use. Spare ribs are the plate of ribs located at the sternum. They are called St. Louis style if the cartilage of the sternum is removed. Baby back ribs come from under the loin muscle. They have more meat than spare ribs but, to my mind, not as much flavor.

Tip: The cooking of ribs is something that is taken very seriously. Some people devote their lives to this task. So, naturally, everyone has an opinion, quite likely strongly held, at that. Ribs are best when cooked long and slow, so that the fat and collagen melt into the meat, which then takes on a spoon-tender texture.

Lamb

I prefer to cook lamb to medium, as I think this is when the flavors come into balance. Rare lamb tends to sacrifice the gamy flavor, as cooking matures the meat and draws out its character, and for the price, you might as well be eating beef. At medium rare to medium, the flavors develop and the fat is given the chance to infuse the meat with its unique aroma. Cooking lamb past medium can cause it to dry out. Keep in mind that lamb fat is highly flavored and should be trimmed significantly before cooking.

Chops (ribs)

This is an elegant and delicious cut. The small bones and half-dollar-size muscle make these fun to eat but tough to cook properly. The chops come from an eight-bone section of ribs that begins at either the fourth or fifth rib and continues toward the hind. If the lamb is very small, the rack of ribs can be left whole or split into two sections of four ribs. Larger racks are often cut into one-bone chops with much of the fat trimmed.

Tip: Don't trim all the fat from the rib! Lamb chops are meant to be a little fatty; that is just part of the cut. To my mind, the best part of the dish is when you get to gnaw on the bones for the last remaining morsels interspersed with charred fat and gristle. If you're cooking racks of lamb, place them bone side down to the fire so as to cook evenly. The meat does not need to be seared; the flavor in lamb develops well through gentle heat.

Loin

Beginning at the last or second-to-last rib, the loin continues to the leg, where it is separated. The loin includes a lot of trim fat and meat, so it is a fairly expensive cut when butchered to a clean, presentable portion. It can be prepared as boneless loins 6 to 8 inches in length or cut across the bone with a saw to make loin chops, some of which will include a portion of the tenderloin much like a beef T-bone steak.

Tip: The loins are extremely lean of marbled fat and cook quickly. It doesn't take long for lamb to dry out when cooked past medium, so be careful with your investment! A brief turn over the direct heat of the fire is welcome, but the majority of the cooking should be done over slow and gentle heat.

Leg

The hind leg of lamb is possibly the most versatile part of any land animal. It contains five different muscles, each with their own character and subtle flavor variations. You often find lamb leg sold with the bones removed, which is quite convenient and recommended. But if you are feeling up to a challenge, ask for one bone-in. There is no better cut of meat for learning butchery than the lamb leg, so take a stab at it, literally.

Tip: The leg can be prepared in numerous ways on the grill. It can be boned and tied into a roast, seared, and then slowly cooked away from the coals. It can also be cut into individual steaks or butterflied and given a deep char over the coals. Leg of lamb takes well to marinades or dry rubs, but not to brining. Anchovy and lamb make for near-perfect partners. The anchovy amplifies the flavor of the lamb and serves to tone down the richness of the fat. See page 268 for Anchovy Marinade.

Top round

Within the leg of lamb, this is a single muscle that makes for a great whole grilled cut or individual steaks. The top round is sometimes sold separately and is very flavorful but very lean. These usually weigh in at 1½ pounds and are easy to cook whole; they make for a great presentation when carved tableside.

Tip: This is worth cooking slowly on the grill after an overnight marinade. The difficulty with the cut is that the grain can be quite confusing, and if you cut it wrong after cooking, it can be distractingly chewy. So orient yourself to the grain before cooking and prepare a strategy so you can identify the proper angle at which to cut when it comes off the grill.

Shoulder

Lamb shoulder is a complicated hunk of meat. The shoulder is capable of a wide array of motion and includes many different muscles, their grains running in all directions. On larger animals, it is worth the reward to remove some of the more tender cuts, but on the tiny lamb, it is a Sisyphean task. I like long cooking for the shoulder, allowing the flavorful heat of a smoky fire to penetrate and soften the fibrous meat.

Tip: Shoulder can be tied into roasts and slowly barbecued, sliced into steaks for a quick grill, or ground into patties. The steaks can give your jaw a workout, but the exercise is well worth the flavor. These steaks must be cut very thin, though, something best done by a butcher with access to a band saw.

The Steak (a.k.a. "Meat Bacon")

I learned how to make this steak from the amazing Carole Greenwood, a chef celebrated as much for her personality as her cooking. She is a genius and the most intuitive cook I have ever known; I learned more in the short period I worked for her than anywhere else. It was Carole who introduced me to the wood grill and the elusive mastery of fire. Preparing this steak requires a sailor-like awareness of everything: the wind or lack thereof, the temperature, humidity, airflow to the grill, the changing heat of the coals, the density and composition of the wood, the grain and personality of the protein, an intuitive understanding of the doneness of the meat. And patience. But stick with it, and you will be rewarded with what I believe to be the best steak you will ever put in your mouth. The end result will have a charred, crispy crust that contrasts deliciously with the evenly cooked, rich, silken flesh. The only garnish or sauce worthy of this steak would be a sprinkling of the Tarragon White Balsamic Condiment (page 278) or Grilled Lemons (page 284).

One 20-ounce NY strip steak cut from the rib end, first or second cut only (see page 216), kept refrigerated

Kosher salt if cooking grain-fed beef or ¼ cup Grass-Fed Beef Grill Salt (page 265) if cooking grass-fed beef

2 cups red wine

2 cups soy sauce

Build a large fire (see page 15) and let it burn down to coals, about 45 minutes. As soon as you start the fire, season the chilled steak very generously on both sides, using kosher salt for grain-fed beef or the grill salt for grass-fed beef. Let the meat sit at room temperature until the fire is ready. Mix the wine and soy sauce in a baking dish big enough to hold the steak and the liquid, and set aside.

When the fire is ready, add 5 or 6 fist-size wood chunks (I like apple wood the best for this, but any wood on the lighter side will work; mesquite or hickory will be too strong.) Allow the wood to flame and then wait 5 minutes.

Sear the steak directly over the coals until it is deeply charred, about 4 minutes. Flip the steak and sear the other side until it too is charred, about 4 minutes. Remove the steak to the pan of marinade, coating it on both sides. Cover the grill and choke the airflow to kill the flames and slow the fire to a heavily smoking smolder.

Place the meat on the grill away from the fire. Cover the grill. After 1 minute, remove the cover and dip the steak on both sides in the marinade again. Then return it to the same place on the grill, flipping it; then replace the cover.

Repeat this process every 45 seconds to a minute for 30 to 40 minutes, depending on the intensity of the heat. Each time you dip, remember to flip, and keep the grill covered when the steak is on the grate. If necessary, add a few more wood chunks to keep the fire smoking heavily.

Cook the steak to your liking (I suggest medium rare). The steak is medium rare when it feels slightly firm if poked with your finger and when the center no longer bulges out if you squeeze it from the sides. You can also test it with an instant-read thermometer; it should register 125 degrees F in the thickest part (but after all that work, it just seems sacrilege to puncture the meat and release a torrent of delicious juices). Remove the steak from the grill and let it rest standing on its narrow side or on a wire rack for at least 15 minutes.

After the meat has rested, slice it no more than ¼-inch thick; I prefer ⅛-inch-thick slices. Do not saw the steak. Rather, set the base of a long, thin slicing knife on the beef and draw it through in one clean motion. Do not trim or remove any of the charred fatty pieces—try one, and you'll know why. Serve immediately.

Serves 4

BLACK AND BLUE STEAK

Restaurant cooks often complain about customers who "don't know how to eat." I used to think that too. I prefer a medium-rare steak, and it would offend me when a guest asked for the steak that I had so carefully selected to be cooked well done. But I always made sure that my cooks took just as much care with that steak as with any other. I taught them it's not our place to judge people by how they prefer their food. Every time a steak was ordered triple killed, I would make sure to watch that plate go from the guest to the dish pit. And for each of those steaks ordered in great offense to my culinary sensibility, the plate would come back empty.

It took me a while, but I got it. As a chef, I serve you. If your plate comes back empty, and you come back to my restaurant next week, then I have done my job, despite my preferences on steak temperatures. This is important to understand.

Food is the most subjective topic there is. As restaurateurs, chefs, cooks, and waitstaff, as hosts in our own homes, we like to think we know best. We seek adulation and confirmation of our efforts. But what pleases one may offend another. There is no situation in which my preferences have any more merit than yours. So order your steak as *you* like.

Enter the "black and blue" steak, also known as "Pittsburgh style." First, a little history. As I understand it, Pittsburgh steel workers would bring raw steak to work and cook it on the surface of the smelter, which was holding molten metal at a temperature of 2,000-plus degrees F. The inside of the meat would not have time to rise even a few degrees before the surface of the steak was blackened and burned. Flipping the steak to cook the other side required asbestos forearms. And so from necessity was born tradition, the black and blue: black because it is burned, blue because it is raw on the inside.

There is no way to achieve this on a conventional grill. Simple science—the fire cannot get hot enough. The closest you may come is to season and then partially freeze your steak (and make it a thick one), then sear it directly over to the hottest fire your grill can manage. Once seared on both sides, allow the meat to defrost, a resting period of a very different kind. Then slice and serve.

Pittsburgh-style requires very flavorful beef, because all the flavor is going to be coming from the beef. Choose only the very best lean cuts of grass-fed beef and season them well in advance to allow even distribution throughout the meat.

Lemon-Crusted Beef Tenderloin

While I very much like the flavor, texture, and beautiful presentation of filet mignon, I eat beef rarely and so often choose the more robustly flavored rib eye or one of the hanging cuts. I do, however, think that filet mignon's perfectly round medallions can be a real treat, though the meat needs a little coaxing. Hence the citrus crust. Really good-quality grass-fed beef is marvelous paired with a sweet/sour component such as the charred lemons here. It helps to amplify the subtle flavors of the meat and to lengthen the interest of the flavors on the palate.

Four 6-ounce portions beef tenderloin

2 teaspoons dried oregano

Kosher salt

Freshly ground black pepper

1 lemon, sliced into super-thin rounds

1 tablespoon extra-virgin olive oil

Build a medium fire in a grill (see page 15); when it has burned down to coals, add chunks of the fruitwood of your choice.

Season the medallions with the oregano and salt and pepper to taste. Let sit for 10 minutes to allow the salt to be absorbed by the meat. Arrange two or three rounds of lemon on one broad side of each medallion so they completely cover that side of the meat. A little overlap is okay. Drizzle with the olive oil and let sit for 20 minutes at room temperature.

Cook the medallions, lemon side down, just adjacent to the coals until the lemons are well charred, 5 to 8 minutes. Using a thin spatula, flip the medallions, making sure to keep the lemon slices attached, and shift them to the coolest part of the grill. Cover the grill and cook until the meat reaches the desired degree of doneness, another 6 to 10 minutes.

Let the medallions rest for 10 minutes before serving. Drizzle them with a light dash of olive oil once plated.

Serves 4

GRILLING LARGE

When you're cooking for a crowd, it is often difficult to execute individual portions of steak perfectly. You have limited fire, so searing the steaks over high heat to create the charred flavor is a real estate challenge. Then you need to slowly roast the meat over a soulful fire to tender perfection. Try to do that with eight individual steaks! The fire loses heat, there's not enough grill space, and so on.

The solution? Cook one large steak, or two if necessary. One or two large strip steaks or rib eyes can be seared over the hottest heat, then moved to absorb slowly smoldering heat. This gives you much more control and takes better advantage of the fire at hand—and you still get the carnal pleasure of watching a giant slab of meat sizzling away near a dancing fire. A thicker steak is easier to cook to your preferred degree of doneness; a thin steak can progress from medium rare to well done in the blink of an eye. With one super-large steak, there is also less fussing about with flipping and tongs, which means it has more time under the cover of the grill absorbing smoke.

A thick steak allows better control over portion size too. And, believe it or not, it's cheaper. If you're going to serve individual steaks, they have to be thick enough to sear without cooking through. That means about 8 ounces per person if you are talking strip steak, 10 to 12 ounces for a rib eye. When a large steak is grilled beautifully, heady with aroma, rested properly, and thinly sliced, you can satisfy your guests with as little as 3 to 5 ounces of meat per person. You also create a sense of communal sharing and a bigger appetite for the delicious side dishes that are really the stars!

THE INS AND OUTS OF FAT

Many cookbooks and chefs wax on about fatty steaks and how they retain moisture. Roasts, yes. Steaks? I say no. As heat is applied and fat melts and drips, it can create a protective layer around the meat, lubricating the mouthfeel and promoting even browning while preventing moisture loss. Sounds good, right? Well, it depends on where that fat is melting. On a roast, the fatty side usually faces upward during cooking so that it does in fact do all these good things. But on a steak, the fat is only on one side and drips down, into the fire; this only promotes massive flare-ups, which will incinerate your expensive piece of meat.

So, please, trim your steaks nearly all the way to the meat, or ask your butcher to do this. This outer fat adds nothing to the culinary delight of the meal and, in fact, is only capable of preventing the proper cooking of it. And request that the piece of fat known as the "lip" be removed. This is that inch-long or longer nugget of fat that extends beyond the meat. You are probably not going to eat it so why pay for it?

Marbling is the kind of fat that you do want in a steak. Notice that I said "in" a steak, not "on" a steak. This type of fat is intramuscular, thin flecks of white fat integrated right into the flesh of quality steaks, much like the beautiful swirling you see in marble, hence the name. This creates a softer and more tender mouthfeel as it melts and helps give the meat a richer, deeper flavor. It's the degree of marbling that determines whether a steak is graded prime, choice, select, etc. The more marbling, the more tender the meat—to a point. A steak should be meaty, not fatty. Wagyu or Kobe beef is prized for its marbling, but to my mind it has crossed the line and tastes more like fat than meat.

Be aware that, on the whole, grass-fed steaks will display little marbling. That is the nature of grass-fed beef. Fat is a product of diet and lack of exercise. A cow fed only on grass doesn't store as much excess fat. So marbling is not the Holy Grail, flavor is—always.

Flank Steak with Radicchio and Plum Salad

One of my greatest pleasures is a salad of bitter lettuces. Some folks do not like the sensation of bitter, but I have always found it to be the most interesting of all the flavors (sweet, salty, sour, bitter, and, some argue, umami). Bitter does not make a grand entrance or steal the show. She is the brooding, complicated, hard to read but impossible to ignore guest at any meal. And when bitter is respected, encouraged, and accepted, she begins to reveal an unmatched intensity and liveliness that is all her own.

Back to the meal at hand. This salad combines the crisp, bitter crunch of summer radicchio with the taut texture of sliced plums to provide a flattering companion to grilled flank, a steak with a good deal of personality. Adding parsley and nutmeg softens the dish with their cool and comforting aromas.

1 pound trimmed flank steak

Kosher salt

2 cups red wine

2 tablespoons red wine vinegar

2 tablespoons extra-virgin olive oil

1 large head radicchio, sliced into ½-inch-wide strips

3 plums (just underripe is best), cut in half, pitted, and thinly sliced

Leaves from ½ bunch fresh flat-leaf parsley

Freshly grated nutmeg

Season the meat with salt. Let it sit at room temperature for at least 20 minutes.

Place the steak on the grill directly over a medium fire (see page 15) and cook for 1 minute per side. Move the steak so it is as far away from the heat as possible. Cover the grill and cook for 8 minutes, then flip the steak and cook for another 4 minutes. Depending on the heat of your fire, the steak should be about medium rare at this point. If this is the desired doneness for you (which I recommend), remove it and let it rest for at least 10 minutes. If you prefer your steak cooked longer, figure on another 4 minutes for medium, 7 for medium well, and 10 for well done, but remember that these times are approximate, depending on the unique heat of your fire.

Meanwhile, combine the wine and vinegar in a small saucepan. Boil over high heat until it has reduced to 3 to 4 tablespoons. Remove it from the heat and whisk in the olive oil.

To serve, mix the radicchio, plums, and parsley in a medium bowl. Season with a little salt and toss to combine. Arrange the salad on a large platter. Using a very sharp knife, slice the steak on a slight bias against the grain. Fan the steak slices around the plate. Drizzle the vinaigrette over the salad and steak and then sprinkle a few gratings of nutmeg (you can use a nutmeg grater or Microplane for this) over the top. Serve immediately.

Serves 4

Chimichurri Marinated Short Ribs

In Argentina, it is rare to escape a meal without having encountered the ubiquitous sauce called chimichurri. It is usually a purée or paste of fresh herbs spiked with chiles and garlic and rounded with olive oil, but you can find thousands of variations, each a reflection of the individual cook preparing it.

While short ribs are rarely seen as anything but a braised dish in America, giving them a quick turn over smoky heat results in a pleasantly chewy and deeply soulful dish. And I really like the way that the marinade caramelizes and chars to form a delicious crust on this decadently fatty and luxuriantly rich meat. The lingering spice helps to accentuate the meaty flavors of the ribs and cut the fat. The meal is best when cooked to medium.

1 large yellow onion, cut into 1-inch chunks

1 clove garlic, peeled

1 bunch fresh cilantro, roots trimmed

1 serrano or jalapeño pepper, cut in half and seeded

2 tablespoons kosher salt

2 tablespoons extra-virgin olive oil

2 pounds bone-in short ribs, cut in 3- to 4-inch pieces

Place the onion, garlic, cilantro, chile pepper, salt, and olive oil into a food processor and pulse until it is a thick paste. Place the short ribs in a zip-top plastic bag, add the herb paste, seal, and massage the paste into the ribs until they are evenly coated. Refrigerate for at least 8 hours and up to 2 days. Let the ribs come to room temperature before cooking; this requires about 30 minutes out of the refrigerator.

Build a medium fire in a grill (see page 15); when it has burned to embers, add hearty wood chips, such as hickory or mesquite. Place the ribs directly over the coals and cover the grill. Close the air vents to a sliver and cook for 5 minutes.

Rotate the grill grates so that the ribs are away from the fire and flip each rib. Cover and cook until the meat against the bone registers 135 degrees F on an instant-read thermometer, about another 10 minutes. Transfer the ribs to a platter and let rest for 10 minutes before serving.

Serves 4

The Hamburger

The quintessential all-American grilled food—a dish so iconic that it nearly defines the backyard cookout. But all too often, the hamburger is treated with indifference by the grill master, if not outright abuse. In fact, it is because I have been served so many terrible burgers that I now usually avoid them and hit the side dishes hard. A good burger should be treated with the care we give to steaks. To me, a hamburger is a very flavorful version of steak—the straightforward taste of beef highlighted by subtle seasonings and best enjoyed as is, nearly unadorned. But this is not what burgers have become. They are lathered in ketchup and relish and mustard and mayonnaise and cheese and bacon, and, and, and. Why? Because insipid tasting meat, ground who knows when, underseasoned, is then pressed and squeezed to push out all juice and flavor as it is being cooked to death. No wonder we pile on the toppings.

It doesn't have to be this way. I will walk you through some very simple steps to create a burger that is everything it should be. Once you have accomplished this, you can add what you like to make it your way.

234

1. Grind your own meat. This is not hard to do and gives you a huge amount of control over the final product. Also, it's kind of fun and makes the process that much more rewarding. I know many cooks who take great pride in making their own pasta, rolling out their own pie dough, pickling the season's bounty. But many of these same cooks have never even considered grinding their own meat. Start with whole cuts of good-quality meat. I think chuck makes the best-tasting and most-flavorful burgers for the dollar. Some high-end chefs are famous for making their burgers from a mix of wagyu beef short ribs, rib eye, strip steak, and other expensive cuts. Some even mix in foie gras. This is unnecessary.

Ask your butcher for a large chuck roast, allowing about 8 ounces of meat per burger. The meat should be trimmed but not entirely denuded of fat. Cut it into 1-inch chunks, removing any visible sinew or slippery fat. The ratio of fat in the chuck, depending on the animal and the section of chuck you get, is about 80/20, perfect for burgers, as far as I'm concerned. Any leaner, and the burgers will lack flavor and won't be able to absorb as much tasty grill smoke. Any fattier, and your burgers will start to taste greasy.

I season the beef once it has been cubed. There is great debate over this, as grinding will exacerbate salt's effect. Simply said, I find that the flavor of presalted ground beef is incomparably better than that of burgers salted just before grilling. Season the meat lightly, about 2 teaspoons kosher salt per pound of meat. If you're using grass-fed beef, you may want to use the Grass-Fed Beef Grill Salt on page 265. In that case, use 4 teaspoons per pound of meat. Toss to evenly distribute and then put the meat into the freezer for 30 minutes. Also place all the parts of the grinder that will touch the meat into the freezer.

Set up your grinder fitted with the large die. Pass the cold cubed meat and fat through the machine as quickly as you can to avoid warming the product. The meat should be extruded in clean streams or large granular pieces. If it is smashing or looks pasty, stop the grinder and examine

the blade and the die. This is usually caused by sinew or fat wrapping around the blade. Remove and discard these strands. Continue to grind until all the meat has passed through. Clean the blade and then grind the beef again using a medium die. Some people prefer to "progressively grind" meat for burgers, meaning that they grind once on a large and then again with a medium die, and even a third time with a small die. This gives the ground meat a smoother, creamier texture. But I like to keep the grind at medium; this way the meat retains a slight grain and chew but is still tender and fully ground. At the very end of grinding, grab a small handful of the double-ground meat and put it through the machine a third time. This will push out any meat remaining in the grind cylinder, ensuring a completely consistent product with no unground pieces. Cover the meat surface with plastic wrap and chill in the fridge.

2. Age the beef. Many people say to use the ground right away, but I prefer to let it rest for at least a few hours, and preferably a whole day. While freshly ground beef is certainly tasty, giving it a little time to breathe is a good thing. When you grind, you greatly increase the surface area exposed to air. Myoglobin, a protein that carries oxygen and iron, reacts rapidly with air, causing a dramatic, and tasty change in the flavor of the beef. Grass-fed beef contains more iron than grain-fed because of the activity level of the animals; this results in a characteristic mineral taste. Allowing between a few hours and up to a day of rest will help to harmonize the flavor and soften the earthy, mineral qualities.

3. Form the patties. Measure out the beef into 6-ounce balls and flatten them into disks. These should be at least 1 inch thick to allow more time for the burger to absorb flavor on the grill. Hamburgers have a tendency to puff up in the center as they cook. To prevent this, press your fingers into the center of the patty to create a dimple.

4. Cook the burgers. A proper fire is the key to a good burger. Get the charcoal burned down to shimmering orange coals, then add wood chunks. I prefer a stronger wood for burgers, such as hickory, oak, or maple. When the wood has caught fire and the flames have subsided to just a flicker above the coals, it is time to cook. Season the patties with a moderate amount of kosher salt. Place the burgers adjacent to the coals and let cook until they begin to brown—not char, brown. Flip the burgers and cook for an equal amount of time. Flip the burgers two more times in this manner to ensure that they cook evenly, the heat penetrating slowly from both sides. I do not provide specific times here, as it would be impossible for me to be accurate, given all the variables involved. Use an instant-read thermometer to check the burgers after the second flip and gauge how much longer to cook them to your preferred doneness. See temperatures for beef on page 216.

Do not ever push, mash, or handle the burgers roughly. Use a spatula and treat them as delicately as possible. Remove the burgers from the grill, place them immediately on the bottom half of a buttered grilled bun, and let them rest for at least 4 minutes. Serve with your chosen condiments and enjoy.

Condiments

A burger cooked by this method will not need to be accosted by sauces of varying sorts. It will be worth eating just as it is, on a bun. As for the bun, if you can get them, use brioche rolls. But whatever the bun, slather it with butter and grill it until crisp before adding the hamburger.

If you're going to use cheese, the colder, the better. Melted cheddar or blue cheese adds nothing to the texture of a burger; in fact, I think it detracts. It also feels greasy. But cold cheese is very different. A pile of shredded cheddar on top of a burger straight off the grill is a textural dream. At first you bite through the soft outer bun, then hit the crisp-toasted buttered side. You then encounter a cool, toothsome, tangy layer of cheese. Proceeding on, the hot, smoky, juicy burger explodes with heat and flavor, finishing with the crisp bun. Wow! Great flavor and a magnificent temperature and textural contrast.

Lettuce simply has no place on a burger. What is it supposed to achieve? It wilts under the heat of the burger and becomes a soggy mush. It reduces the structural integrity of the burger/bun edifice, almost guaranteeing a messy last few bites. If you must have lettuce, try frisée or arugula. Both will suffer the same complications but will at least add flavor. Tomatoes are a different story. A thick, juicy slice of a giant Cherokee Purple or peach-colored Candy Stripe heirloom tomato is wonderful. It will present some structural difficulty, but in this case its flavor is worth the mess. If the tomato isn't amazing on its own, though, it will only detract from the burger, so don't bother if it isn't good.

Onions are another repeat offender in the normal burger routine. Usually it is one large cross-section of an onion that was cut hours, if not days ago. Onions are too powerful to use raw more than 20 to 30 minutes after being cut. And I find that an onion cut in cross-section is even more potent than when sliced laterally. The crunch can be quite nice, but only a little bit is needed to make a big difference. Try thinly slicing the onion laterally and placing just a few pieces on the bun under the burger for maximum texture. They will wilt slightly but still retain crunch, and they'll soften in flavor. Red onions are preferable to the conventional yellow.

Whether or not to use sauces is up to you. However, homemade mayonnaise or Herb Mayonnaise is mighty tasty (page 68).

SIMPLE ★ SUSTAINABLE ★ DELICIOUS

GRILLING

WHERE THERE'S SMOKE